MYTHOLOGY OF STONE

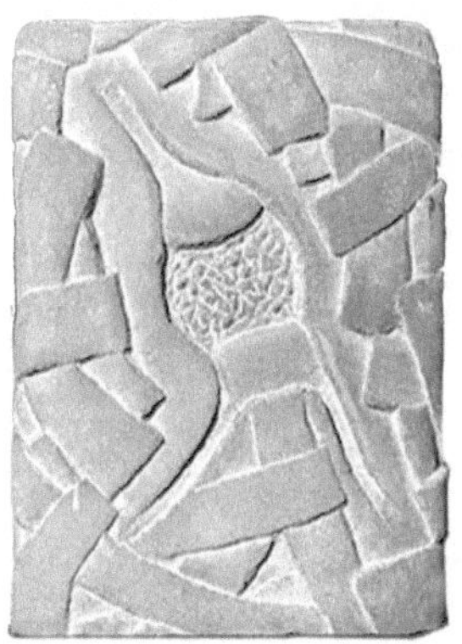

BRADFORD GRAVES

Curated by
VERNA GILLIS

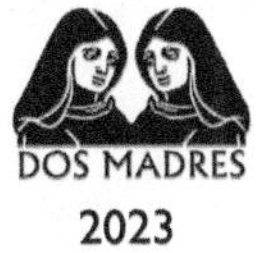

2023

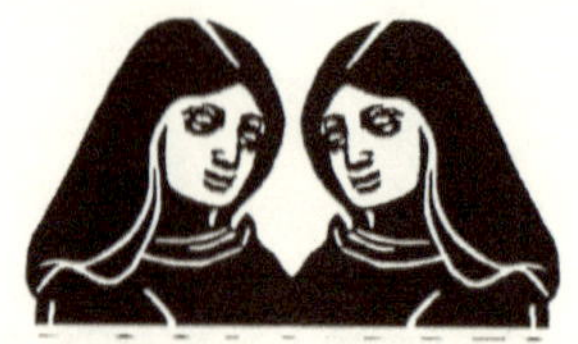

DOS MADRES PRESS INC.
P.O. Box 294, Loveland, Ohio 45140
www.dosmadres.com editor@dosmadres.com

Dos Madres is dedicated to the belief that the small press is essential to the vitality of contemporary literature as a carrier of the new voice, as well as the older, sometimes forgotten voices of the past. And in an ever more virtual world, to the creation of fine books pleasing to the eye and hand.

Dos Madres is named in honor of Vera Murphy and Libbie Hughes, the "Dos Madres" whose contributions have made this press possible.

Dos Madres Press, Inc. is an Ohio Not For Profit Corporation and a 501 (c) (3) qualified public charity. Contributions are tax deductible.

Executive Editor: Robert J. Murphy

Illustration & Book Design: Elizabeth H. Murphy
www.illusionstudios.net

Cover: November Steps IV. 1998,
Bluestone and Limestone by Bradford Graves

"The Question—What is Your Hope?" David Smith, 1947
used with permission from the David Smith Estate

Typeset in Adobe Garamond Pro
ISBN 978-1-953252-91-3
Library of Congress Control Number: 2023944070

First Edition

Published by Dos Madres Press, Inc.

ACKNOWLEDGEMENTS

Deep gratitude to John Taggart and Michael Heller for their continuing support and consistent help with getting this manuscript published.

To Dos Madres Press for continuing to publish and birth the book as an object.

To Ivan Rubenstein-Gillis for editing the manuscript and to Kristen Holt-Browning for copyediting.

Gratitude and our shared connection for Brad's work to Elizabeth Murphy for her beautiful design and to Robert Murphy for everything else. And to their two mothers.

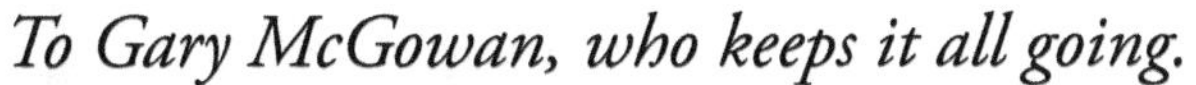

To Gary McGowan, who keeps it all going.

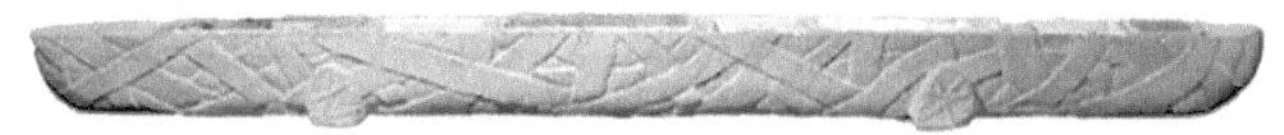

TABLE OF CONTENTS

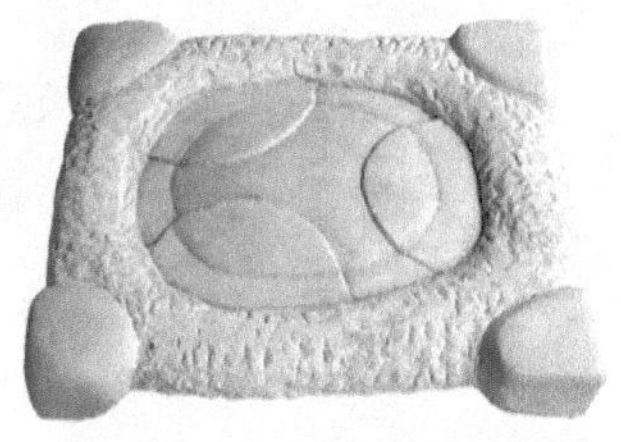

MYTHOLOGY OF STONE

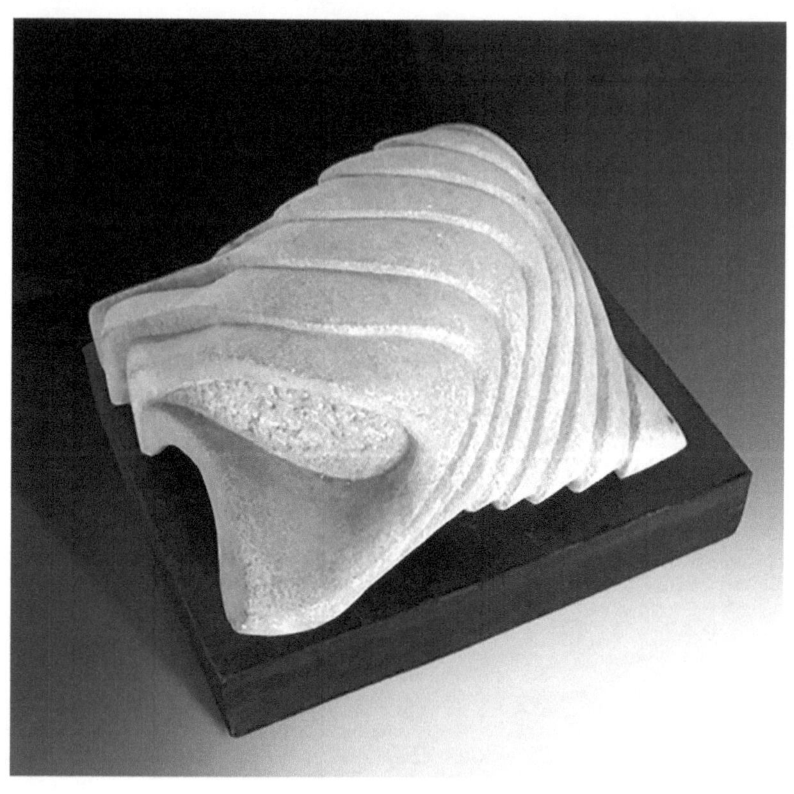

INTRODUCTION

Thinking about how best to introduce the writings of Bradford Graves, the realization dawned that it couldn't be done properly without taking our friendship into account. A distanced "third person" commentary would be a false presentation. I must ask for some understanding, then, as to why I mention myself frequently and refer to the sculptor as "Brad."

I encountered his work before I met its maker. That was "Trane," which was brought to my attention by the poet Michael Heller. This was 1968–1969, when I was putting together an issue of *Maps*, a poetry magazine, honoring the recently deceased jazz musician John Coltrane. He was the heavyweight champion whose *A Love Supreme* album had become one of *the* major events of the 1960s (and remains so today). The sculpture was of a like size, and its location—in a mountain region of the Czech Republic—reinforced the broad appeal of his music. Obviously, a photo of the sculpture had to go in the issue! It was a powerful testimonial among all the textual testimonials.

And it was jazz and music generally which was the center of our friendship, a co-operation or conversation of poetry and sculpture.

Friends share enthusiasms. One of my own was William Bronk. I had published one of his poems in *Maps* and recommended his work to Brad. This matters because Bronk became something of a seed-crystal for Brad's own work. There are three specific pieces, all from the mid-1970s: *Bronk, An Algebra Among Cats,* and *In Walked Monk.* Of these, the last has personal importance for me.

Brad died of a heart attack in 1998. Some years later his wife, Verna Gillis, relocated his work from the New York City studio to their property in Kerhonkson, NY. During this process she invited me to select a piece for myself. I chose *In Walked Monk.* It took some time to find its right place (no easy task) in the hill and dale countryside of south-central Pennsylvania where my wife and I live. Still later it would become the subject of my poem "Plinth" (*Pastorelles,* 2004).

The sculpture in more detail, beginning with a Bronk seed-crystal. This is his essay on the ancient Peruvian city of Machu Picchu (*The New World* 1974). Very quickly we find what may have caught Brad's attention:

"The terrain and its background have been probed for their best value in much the same way as a piece of stone is said to be studied by the sculptor who intends to develop his conception from it."

And—after describing a ledge situated to form a cave behind it—"... the rock on the right of the eave's entrance is beautifully carved into broad facets in a manner we would now call abstract." This is precisely what we see in another sculpture by Brad, *An Algebra Among Cats* (1975). Which happens, also, to be the title of Bronk's essay.

But it is a later passage from this essay that bears on the *Monk* sculpture. After noting the city's many stairways:

"... there is another rock here, a carved one. Perhaps, cut would be a better word, for it is not ornamental; but the relationship of its planes and surfaces are those of sculpture... Above the broad base, the rock has been shaped to form a blunt, four-sided post."

Even though the Bronk "Algebra" connection may be "close," there's no need for a seed to replicate itself exactly. To begin with, the *Monk* piece consists of a fairly narrow base and *two* widely spaced apart carved pillars or "posts." Further, the base has a carved out irregular channel connecting with the channels carved into the inner face of each pillar. And, of course, any work of art may have more than a single seed. Another possibility is a statement by the sculptor David Smith that Brad quotes in his own "About Sculpture" essay, that is, "I would like to make sculpture *that would rise from water and tower in the air*" (my emphasis). It's of interest that this work, completed one year after the "Algebra" piece, has Kansas limestone *and water* as its listed material.

In the same essay Brad calls attention to all that's involved with siting a sculpture. In particular, "the base-pedestal may be integrated into the sculpture, still maintaining its function as support, but may [also] become the focal point of the sculpture."

What Brad calls base-pedestal is what I designate as plinth. A fact also designated in that poem: even before my selection, the plinth had been broken and would need repair before the sculpture as an interlocked whole (pillars seated in plinth) could be sited "in place." Only then could music "enter as through a welcoming portal." Or the music of Thelonious Monk can't enter—can't walk in or step in—unless there's a welcoming portal of attention. Why the welcoming: because music gives form/order and meaning/value to human life.

In his essay, Bronk emphasizes *the alone* as in his question about how much one person who had always been alone in an uninhabited forest could hear "as an outside sound." This has to do with Machu Picchu, which is "outside of the traditions and descent of Western civilization." He compares looking at the city to hearing a new, utterly foreign language. "Yet not only do we recognize human speech, we hear our own intonations and understand emotional attitudes." Unmentioned by Bronk, there is an answer from one who had always been alone. This is Shakespeare's Caliban: "the isle is full of noises, sounds and sweet airs that give delight and hurt not." Yes, by Western civilization standards, Caliban is not so much a "person" as a creature. As such, he forces the question of just how "civilized" the civilization is: *The Tempest* has a supposedly happy ending, but the tension of nature/culture remains.

There's a version of this tension in Bronk's poem "The Beautiful Wall, Machu Picchu." The first stanza deals with classic Greek sculpture: "This way of handling stone is to say of the world / it is workable, and yielding and full to the hand." The second presents the stones of the "beautiful wall" as "abstract austerities, unimitative." The wall makes "found grace inherent more an idea than in / the world, loved simple soundness in a just joint, / and the pieces together once though elsewhere apart." Point: the "Monk" sculpture has a like quality of construction but makes a doorway—the "empty" space between the two posts —in the wall of Western imitative art so that an "outside" art, jazz, may enter with new sounds that delight and hurt not, as well as offering new meaning/value to our lives.

I will often make mention of crystals and crystallization. They are important terms in Brad's writings. From "The Making of Sculpture": the creative process "is analogous to crystallization." From the conclusion of "About Sculpture": "sculpture should be a process of crystallization" and "every new work should be a new crystal, a new being." This may have some connection with my book *The Pyramid Is a Pure Crystal* (1974). A more direct linkage is with the French sculptor Jean Arp. That is, sculpture as human concretions, the result of a process of crystallization, and as indications that "something has grown." At the same time, it should be noticed that Brad's work shows little if any resemblance to that of Arp.

It's a late recognition on my part of what Brad was doing in a series of drawings for my *Peace on Earth* book (1981). Specifically for the paperback edition cover: the pillars or posts of the *Monk* sculpture are turned into four-sided tall crystals. In a sense, the stone is identical to the pen and ink drawing. What makes them truly different, though, is our angle of vision. We can't see all four sides or faces from any single position when viewing the sculpture, but we can with the drawing. The book contains four poems. There is a separate drawing facing the first page of each poem. The four internal drawings don't simply repeat the cover, but each shows a progressive metamorphosis rendering what was hard/crystalline into the fluid and flowing. They are much more than merely "illustrations."

Easily enough, beyond sharing and enthusiasm, we can understand why Brad found Bronk to be a stimulating source. For the terms of what's found praiseworthy in "The Beautiful Wall" are essentially what's to be found in the "constructivist" manifestos of such pioneering but now famous sculptors such as Barbara Hepworth in the 1930s publication *Circle*. Yet there is an important difference. Walls can be beautiful in themselves; they can also offer protection and privacy, some individual self space. Bronk hints at this in his "For an Early Italian Musician" poem. It is a sonnet with two wishes: to be complete and to last. They can only be accomplished "by a slow / crystal on crystal accretion of a made / world, a world made to last."

Crystals again, yes, but Bronk makes no allowance for an opening, a literally open space which makes possible the entry of the outside, especially that which is outside any tradition we're born into and naturally accept as authority. Monk's music, as an instance of the outside, provides the possibility of release from the enslavement of tradition. And, with that, new meaning/value. Not security/stasis but movement and growth.

Brad's attention to music wasn't limited to jazz. For example: Jordi Savall's soundtrack for the 1991 French film *Tous les matins du monde*, which he recommended to me as "the music of paradise." The soundtrack concentrates on works associated with Sainte-Colombe, a 17th-century composer and master of the bass viola. It was a signal of the arrival of old music in the ears of a "modern" audience only now heard as "early music." The signal came by way of period-authentic instruments and performance practices. In a time dominated by "the tradition of the new," this was an exciting *renewed* music performed by expert vocal groups (the Hilliard Ensemble and the Orlando Consort), instrumentalists (Savall himself and the lutenist Paul O'Dette), individual singers (Emma Kirkby), and the conducting of John Eliot Gardner. More than a novelty, early music continues to "delight and instruct" ears that thought they'd already heard everything worth hearing.

Sainte-Colombe plays an important part in my book *When the Saints*. Published in 1999, one year after Brad's death, it is dedicated to him. And not only that music, but also a sculpture by Brad plays an even more important part. This is *Sound Sculpture* (1979), which is also an instrument of his own invention, a stone xylophone. Even as "lithophone" is a more literally correct label, I see it this way to make clear its resemblance to *and* difference from the more familiar instrument.

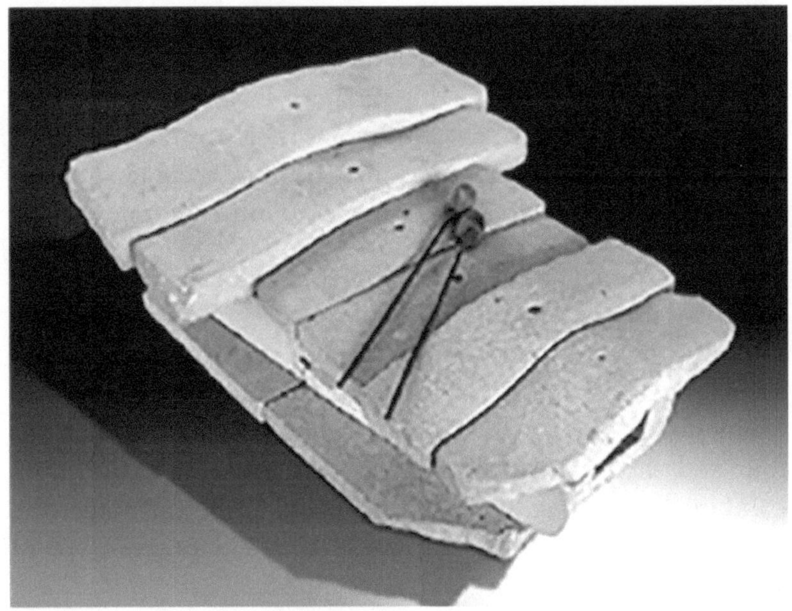

Made of limestone, the sculpture is mounted on two thin stone "planks," the whole supported by a wooden box or tablelike construction painted white. The viewer does not look "at" the sculpture so much as look upon it (at waist level). Its "keyboard" = five separate stones. Each is fitted closely but not uniformly with the other. Each has a small sound hole. Two (*left*) are much larger/longer; three (*right*) are smaller. The larger stones are a pale, light grey. The smaller stones are more beigelike, even faintly rose color. Though very subtle, the colors are made distinct by the contrasting white support.

That stone may be colored should not be surprising. As stated in "About Sculpture": "today, color on any material is accepted as an integral part of the sculpture". Thus color can "strengthen" the sense of a material's very "materiality." It can also "clarify a combination of forms and sharpen the imagery."

The upper surfaces of all the stones are smooth; the bottom edges are rough. Not uniform xylophone "bars," the upper surfaces vary in level or thickness. This variation is, again, very subtle. The stones' shapes may be seen as biomorphic abstractions, but I think Arp's "human concretions" may be more accurate. For this is a sculpture experienced on a close, even intimate scale.

It is also experienced as something else, as an instrument and the possibility of music. The small wooden mallets encourage sounding out the tones of the stones. Even more, to sound them out as separate tones in a certain time sequence – as Monk does at the beginning of "Misterioso," which counts out four and then counts them again (and again). Or the tones combined according to some other tune. (Who can forget the "chanted" rhythm cell of Coltrane's "A Love Supreme"?) *Or* to a new tune of the player's own conception.

What matters is the possibility, the possibility of an order, simple or complex, some order, some concord of sound(s) that delights and hurts not. Something that can be hummed. Simple or complex, what matters is the possibility. This is the ultimate crystal, the clearest of clear gifts.

Now listen to a "fuller" version of Bronk on the "outside" appeal of Machu Picchu:

"It is somewhat as it is when we hear a new language whose words and grammar, or even its very sounds, are entirely foreign to us. Yet not only do we recognize human speech, we hear our own intonations and understand emotional attitudes which are expressed or groped for or dissembled. We can be strongly attracted or repelled without an interpreter. And these ruins are almost more eloquent than language."

Sound Sculpture is not a ruin. Nor are any of the others. And eloquence is not the issue. But Bronk's affirmation of recognition, hearing, and understanding goes beyond delights and hurts not. Or includes both and goes toward a larger possibility of meaning/value, a shared crystallization of human concretion.

The root meaning of "paradise" is "park." It is through the thoughtful care of Verna Gillis that these sculptures can now be seen in their own best place: The Bradford Graves Sculpture Park in Kerhonkson, NY. It is her gift of his gift for all of us.

— JOHN TAGGART

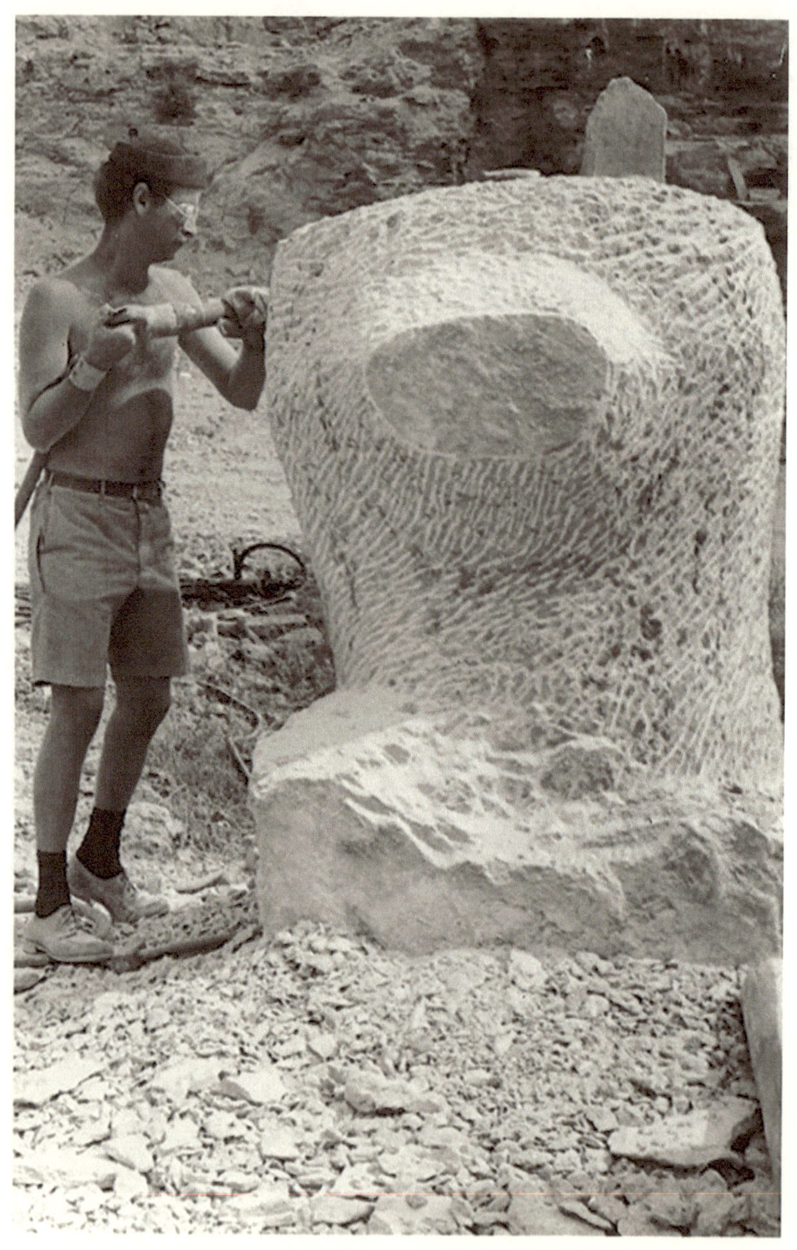

THE MAKING OF SCULPTURE

The making of sculpture may be taken as a desire for wholeness: The recognition of one's identity as part of the earth and its materials. In the confrontation of one's inner image with physical materials, a dialogue begins and the result is a sculptural statement. Through this dialogue an attempt is made to clarify subject and object matter. The subject matter is the discovery, and not how much I know as I fabricate the sculpture. The object matter is the myriad of personal preconceptions that we transfer on to materials. People, cultures, other objects, past events—All become the excess baggage of symbols carried around with us, become the basis of abstract object art. Out of this confrontation, what we look for is the art of "The real." The real is the dialogue between fabricator and his materials, not a dialogue with oneself. One wants to touch, walk the earth, and create a place for events. The material I have chosen to have a working dialogue with is stone. Stone, one of the oldest sculptural materials, not to be confused with its architectural use, has been limited by its outer boundaries, the monolithic block. I have attempted to overcome this by utilizing work methods derived from constructivism, the pitting together of separate blocks allowing space to become an active part of the sculpture. This is a unifying method of working that allows each unit of my sculptures to create its own reasons for existence. The process is analogous to crystallization. First there is the idea, the basis of an internal ordering of structure, expanded or split into different units. From this, the resulting segmentation of a conceptual idea through physical units hints at the crystallization. They become like stars in the night sky, each defined by its own space, but perceived together they make up the fabric of a universe.

—BRADFORD GRAVES, 1939–1998

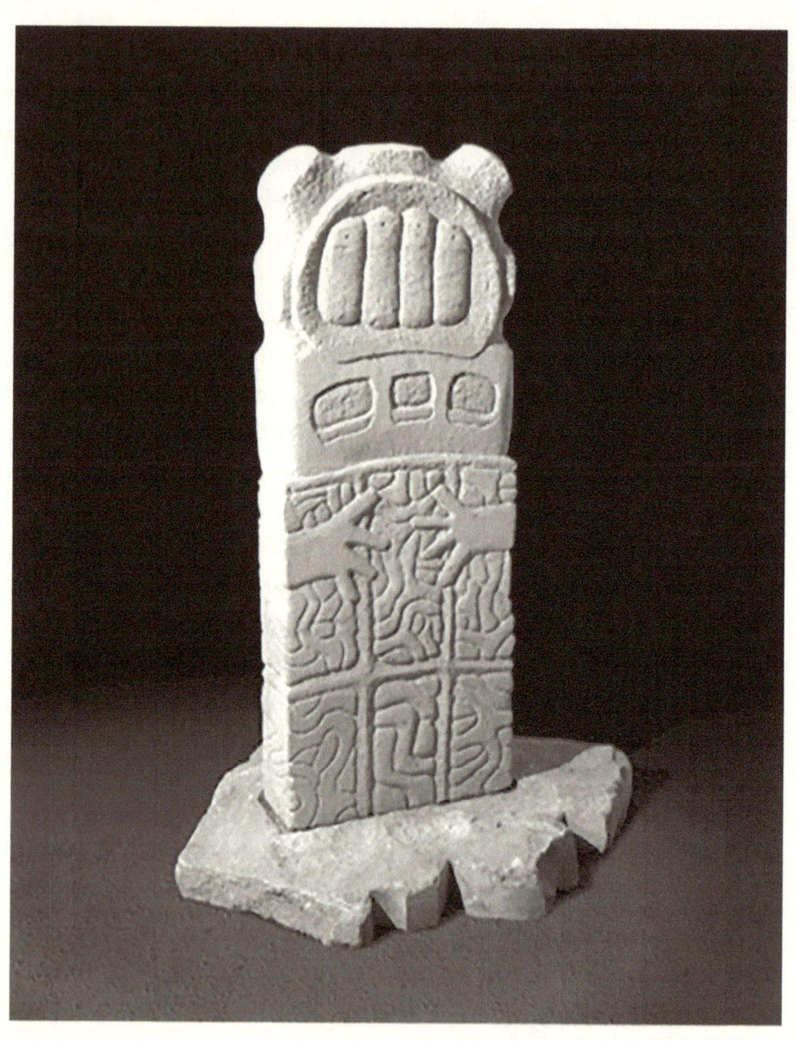

ABOUT SCULPTURE

The problem is having to translate into words what is totally a visual experience. In order to fully comprehend sculpture, a visual, three-dimensional object, it has to be seen. Reading about it isn't going to help that much and photographs are only a slight improvement, since photos are flat images and cannot convey the full, spatial quality of a three-dimensional object. If we read a guide book to the Taj Mahal, it will tell us how to locate the building and find items that are within, but it isn't a substitute for the direct experience of that wonder. It's nice to know where the marble is from, who's buried there, etc., but to experience the art is to feel the rush of space within. I can only hope that I will be able to create an interest in sculpture that will lead the reader to a direct interaction with it.

This paper is a guide. For better or for worse, we have chosen to store and transmit information through the written word, due to its accessibility. However, knowledge is stored not only in the written word but also in visual images and sounds. I can give you certain information on sculpture, but true knowledge can only be found in direct perception of sculpture.

Knowledge—the understanding of what is known—can only be a tool. What I am going to do in the following pages is to help the student of sculpture develop tools to isolate components, to define and extract essentials and to begin to appreciate what sculpture is. The utilization of these tools leads to an intelligent way of looking at sculpture. I do not want to write about what art is, that unknown quantity and quality which is always one step ahead of understanding. Rather, I want to deal with what can be known, that which is universal to all sculpture, such as how the individual parts are put together to make a total statement. What is unique to any piece of sculpture is the way in which these components fit together. That's why each piece of sculpture becomes a separate, emotional experience.

These tools will be used differently by the viewer than the sculptor. The viewer uses these tools as a means to an end, the fullest appreciation of sculpture. The sculptor will challenge these concepts to escape their definition. In fact this is what tradition is—definitions from the past.

We sculptors, students and viewers are all coming from different places, geographically as well as psychologically, bringing with us our baggage of unique perceptions, as well as unique hindrances. For example, the physician who collects Pre-Columbian art because of its graphic representation of ancient diseases is not dealing with the abstract qualities of sculpture. His interest is turned away from the individual art work to what his own information is bringing to the piece. There is a tendency to set up mirrors within us so that we are always perceiving ourselves rather than a new vision.

The difficulty lies in finding a balance between our world within and outside phenomena. Perception should be more than soaking up the world through our immediate senses. We must bring our sensibilities to bear and heighten our ability to conceptualize. The viewer must put as much work into viewing the sculpture as the sculptor did into making it. Viewing has to be more than a passive activity.

Our sense of sight is one of our neglected senses. We are conditioned early in life to rarely use our eyes to see three dimensionally, except in times of personal danger. For example, if I cross the street now, how long will it take the car coming up the road to intersect my path? We use our eyes to gain information from two-dimensional materials such as books, films, television, photos, and everyday directional signs. As a result, we perceive from left to right, but rarely from our body centers away. It is implied that we are passive in between left and right. If we become active, "left or right" ceases to have meaning, and we have entered the realm of the third dimension.

In order to perceive sculpture we will have to become Alice —locate the looking glass, go through it, and like her, find a new world.

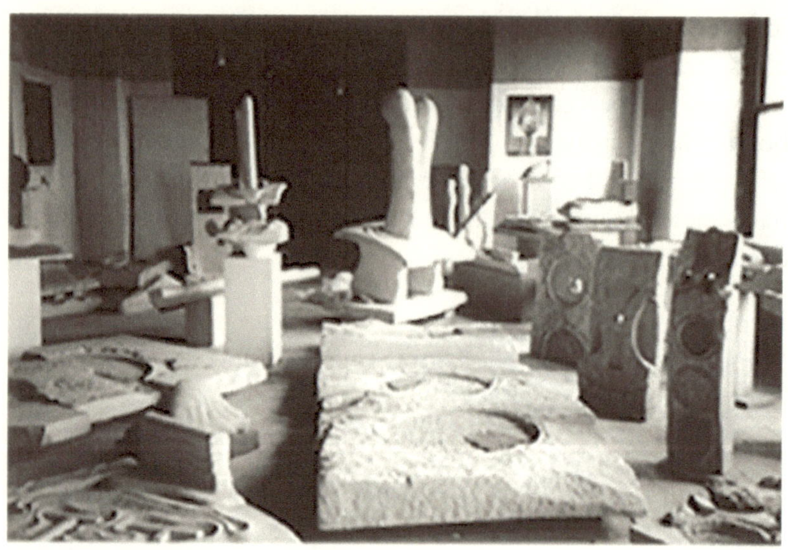

SCULPTURE—A DEFINITION

The making of sculpture may be taken as a desire for the realization of wholeness. We don't want to be on the world, but in it. We begin by putting our identity on materials with the hope that we will become one with the world.

Watch a child handle any material. He will deform, mutilate, or shape the material into a new form. He may take that material and combine it with another material into a structure. Or he may set that material aside from others and give it a personal value. Even when a child is given a toy that already has meaning invested in it by the adult world, the child often will give it meaning in ways unthought of by adults.

The personal meaning given materials by a child is his way of neutralizing and protecting himself from an indifferent environment. By turning materials into an object it becomes something known.

An adult takes up the materials of the earth and works them in order to set up a relationship. An animal feels fear in responding to an unknown thing; it responds to the unknown by staying clear of it, and avoids establishing a connection. But man, in experiencing fear, goes towards the source. He will name it, invent a myth to explain its action, and he will apply this knowledge to his personal welfare. He establishes a relationship which is a kind of wholeness between himself and the source of his fear.

We are not seeking here to understand the source of fear, but rather to attempt to understand the response that is at the beginning of sculpture. Man goes towards a relationship, while an animal goes towards isolation. Man's self-induced fear is the result of his unfulfilled relationship with life. He creates in order to establish a relationship with the world around him.

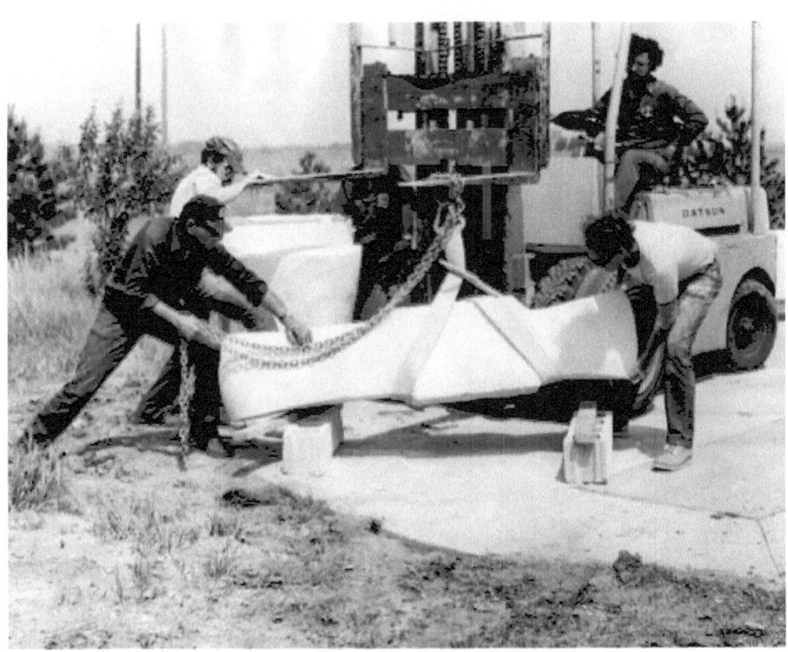

We have the choice of being a human being or a brute being. To experience ourselves, our thoughts and our feelings as something separated from the rest, as a restricted prison, or we may free ourselves from this prison by widening our circle of compassion in the realization that each of us is part of a whole, while the *individual me* inherits the earth for this one split second.

Sculpture has its roots, by way of handicrafts, in manual labor. We cultivated the earth by manual labor in order to survive. The manual work was done in order to transform material into something useful. The interest is placed on the results. With handicrafts, the art is in the enhancement of an object suited for use. The working of matter is developed to reveal its fullest potentials. Man makes matter more significant. Sculpture is significant in man's conceptualizing, with the material remaining in the background.

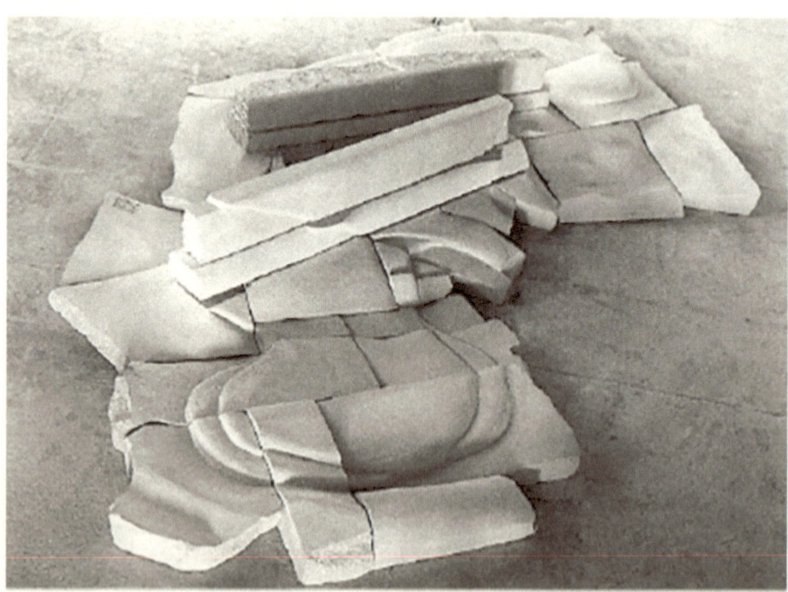

We are still children handling materials, naming and giving a personal value in our relationships. The child applies the universe to himself, and from there goes on to imitation and self-expression. There he has stopped. Most of art has stopped there. The era of a pure art reflecting wholeness hasn't begun yet, but we can make an attempt at a start.

The making of a three-dimensional symbol that relayed information by way of inert material has been the accepted definition of sculpture. Through the evolution of sculpture it had become cluttered with the overlaying of symbolic messages. The history of Western sculpture has been the questioning and dismantling of the accepted idea of what sculpture should be. The concept of sculpture that has emerged is of a non-functioning object that has a life of its own. A sculpture no longer needs to justify itself by subject matter with the forms construed as representational or symbolic. There is a newfound freedom to take the creation of form in any direction.

The Question—What Is Your Hope?

I would like to make sculpture that would rise from
water and tower in the air—
that carried conviction and vision that had not
existed before
that rose from a natural pool of clear water
to sandy shores with rocks and plants
that men could view as natural without reverence or awe
but to whom such things were natural because they were
statements of peaceful pursuit—and joined in the
phenomenon of life
Emerging from unpolluted water at which men could bathe
and animals drink—that

harbored fish and clams and all things natural to it
I don't want to repeat the accepted fact,
moralize or praise the past or sell a product
I want sculpture to show the wonder of man, that flowing water,
rocks, clouds, vegetation, have for the man in peace who
glories in existence
this sculpture will not be the mystical abode
of power of wealth of religion
Its existence will be its statement
It will not be a scorned ornament on a money changer's temple
a house of fear
It will not be a tower of elevators and plumbing with every
room rented, deductions, taxes, allowing for depreciation
amortization yielding a percentage in dividends
It will say that in peace we have time
that a man has vision, has been fed, has worked
it will not incite greed or war
That hands and minds and tools and material made a symbol
to the elevation of vision
It will not be a pyramid to hide a royal corpse from pillage
It has no roof to be supported by burdened maidens
It has no bells to beat the heads of sinners
or clap the traps of hypocrites, no benediction
falls from its lights, no fears from its shadow
this vision cannot be of a single mind—a single concept,
it is a small tooth in the gear of man,
it was the wish incision in a cave,
the devotion of a stone hewer at Memphis
the hope of a Congo hunter
It may be a sculpture to hold in the hand
that will not seek to outdo by bulky grandeur
which to each man, one at a time, offers a marvel of

close communion, a symbol which answers to the holder's vision, correlates the forms of woman and nature, stimulates the recall sense of pleasurable emotion, that momentarily rewards for the battle of being

—DAVID SMITH

Note: "The Question—What Is Your Hope?", from the Estate of David Smith. Original version, Smith notebook 28 (c. 1940s) final version c. 1947.

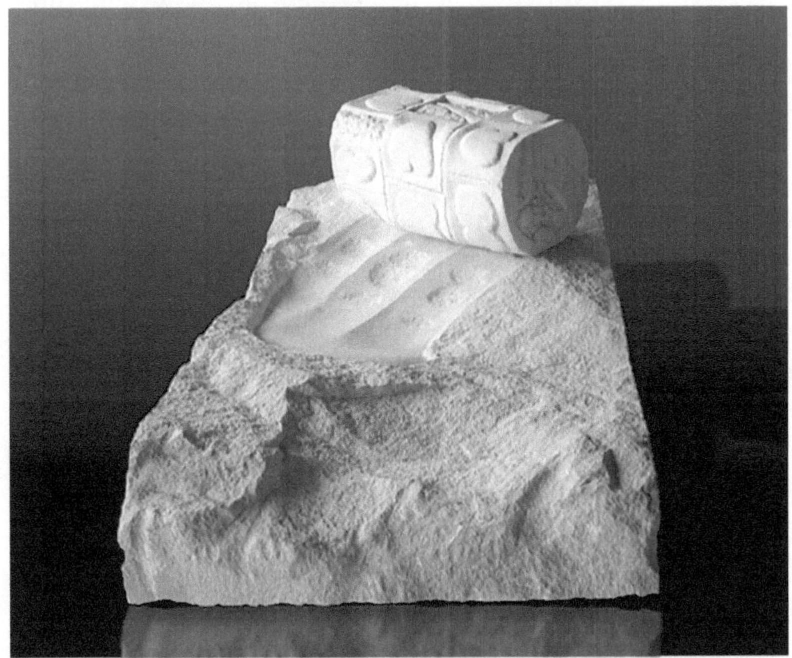

MATERIALS

There are two materials for sculpture. One is the actual physical matter to be worked upon, and the second is the life.

Traditionally, the sculptor had to choose stone, wood, clay, or bronze as his material. Sculpture was expected to survive the ages and had to be realized in hard, durable materials.

Today, the sculptor is able to range over any material that suits the creation of a particular idea. There are now sculptures that are soft and pliable, that readily mold themselves to the environment. The environment itself is a subject for sculpture in which further form change is left to nature's ecology.

The new approach to material was one of the first statements found in modern sculpture. Since the end of the Renaissance until the beginning of the twentieth century, materials had been abused by the sculptor. Works were first done in one material, such as clay, on a small scale, and then transferred to another material such as stone without regard to structure or scale. A sculptor would make an image ten inches high in clay and then a battery of artisans would enlarge that image into stone through the use of measuring tools, and the sculpture would be placed on a site without regard for the visual scale of the final location. Often the sculptor didn't even see the finished piece. Stone sculptures were molded from wet clay. Stone is carved, hard, durable material, not a plastic material that is modeled such as clay. In the nineteenth century, the manufacture of sculpture became dominant, executed by artisans, and the quantity of sculpture produced had an inverse proportion to the quality.

Modern sculpture began with the sculptor reasserting himself with the object and the material. The sculptor worked directly on the material, and with stone this was called "direct stone carving." This meant that the sculptor worked on the stone without having previously made a model in another material, allowing the individual stone to suggest shapes. This is a process that allows the sculptor to improvise as the work progresses.

This led the sculptor to the concept of "Truth to Materials." This meant that each material had a look and feeling that demanded the sculpture to be developed fully in that direction. It became apparent that this placed a limitation on the inception of a piece, and as a concept it went the traditional route of developing into a mystique of materials.

Does stone have a stony look, does wood have a woody look? And what does that even mean? "Truth to materials" is a psychological statement that can change from sculptor to sculptor dealing with man's world, and is not about the nature of material. The only truth that doesn't change is that a sculptor must take into consideration the structural properties of a material.

Material is chosen according to the form of the content. Can the material hold the image? Should the form be hot or cold? You can have a cold image in a natural material such as dead white marble, or a hot form in an industrial material such as a cool plastic. Cold and hot forms depend upon the total configuration of the piece and the relationships of the forms. The crossing of image and material is another reason "truth to materials" is no longer valid. Must a material be defined as "truth" and thus be limited?

A sculptor may select a material and fit his idea to it or he may have an idea and fit the material to it. The first idea is a physical one, and the second, a mental one, but both have the same results. It's important to maintain an open attitude and to experiment, combining or reversing the above two processes with material in a single piece. Soon, the experimental stage between sculptor and material ends, a direction is found, and the experimenting is then, in its turn, left to the viewer. He will then have to devise ways of relating the new materials of sculpture to his concept of what sculpture should be.

As I said at the beginning of this section, the world of the sculptor is also material for sculpture. Each age demands its own art. The art of other ages can give us insights, but no answers. Our age is one of dissolution, and this is the material of our art. The summarizers and reflectors, using dissolution and disorder, create an art not from, but out of, disorder, spreading the process of coming apart. Another approach is to work from the disorder, attempting to fabricate an order that rises to a whole. To maintain a sense of wholeness, a principle of order is required of an artwork. In an age that is going into a state of chaos, the artist must work harder, with a more violent effort, in order to affect his synthesis. He must literally make the plastic form of his vision from the substance of experience without the guide of an aesthetic tradition.

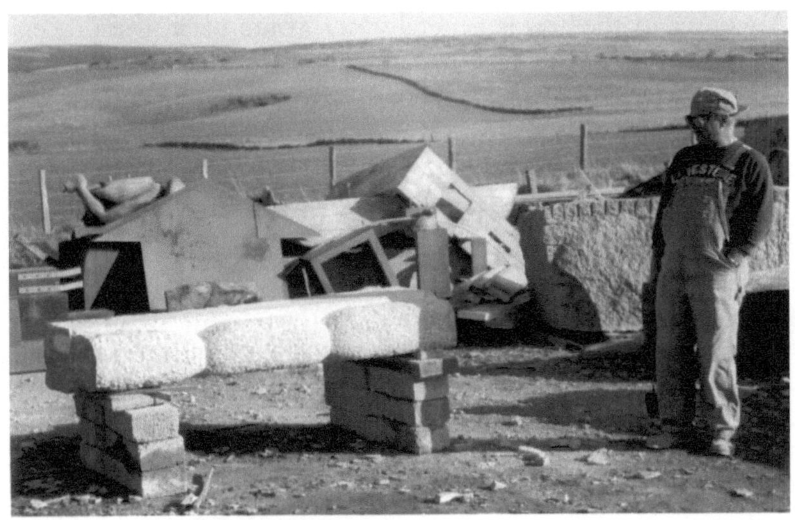

THE HANDLING OF MATERIALS

It has been estimated that approximately 125,000 sculptures are produced each year in the United States. If you add sculpture to the number of commercially produced objects within a year, there comes the realization that we are on the edge of literally drowning in objects. The relation of people to objects has lost its balance so that our lives are beginning to feel cluttered by objects. Our system demands the continuation of the fabrication of objects with a shortened life of use, and as a result things fall apart before our very eyes.

Where does sculpture fit into this? I think more thought should be given to the recyclability of the materials of sculpture.

Not only are we drowning in the debris of broken or unused objects, but we are suffocating from the debris in the air, put there as a result of fabrication. Toxic fumes are released every time materials are altered chemically.

A worker in the arts is generally not aware of all the process changes in materials. He can't afford to hire research assistants, and his nature will lead him to experiment in areas not yet covered by research.

We should know more about materials. Few ceramists know that dangerous fumes are put into the air each time clay and glazes are altered. Many artists working with plastics develop kidney stones or nerve disorders. The chemical alteration in plastic not only puts toxic material into the air, but the resulting material can't be reused by the earth's recycling action. Welding, stone cutting, and paint all release harmful dust and fumes into the air.

Be aware of the consequences of both the working and final outcome of the product. As a stone cutter, while working, I wear protective clothing, steel-tipped shoes, safety glasses, dust mask, earphones to block out high-decibel noise, and gloves. If the stone I am working on breaks, or is no longer needed, it can be returned to the earth. I am always aware of the weights I am working with, up to two tons, and I have the lifting devices, such as an overhead hoist and forklift. Much of the art being created today is an industrial situation so the studio must be set up to handle material on that level. Spend the money on the best equipment and materials. Don't scrimp.

Think through each step with care in the handling of material. The most important and most elusive material on earth is life, and care should be given to it.

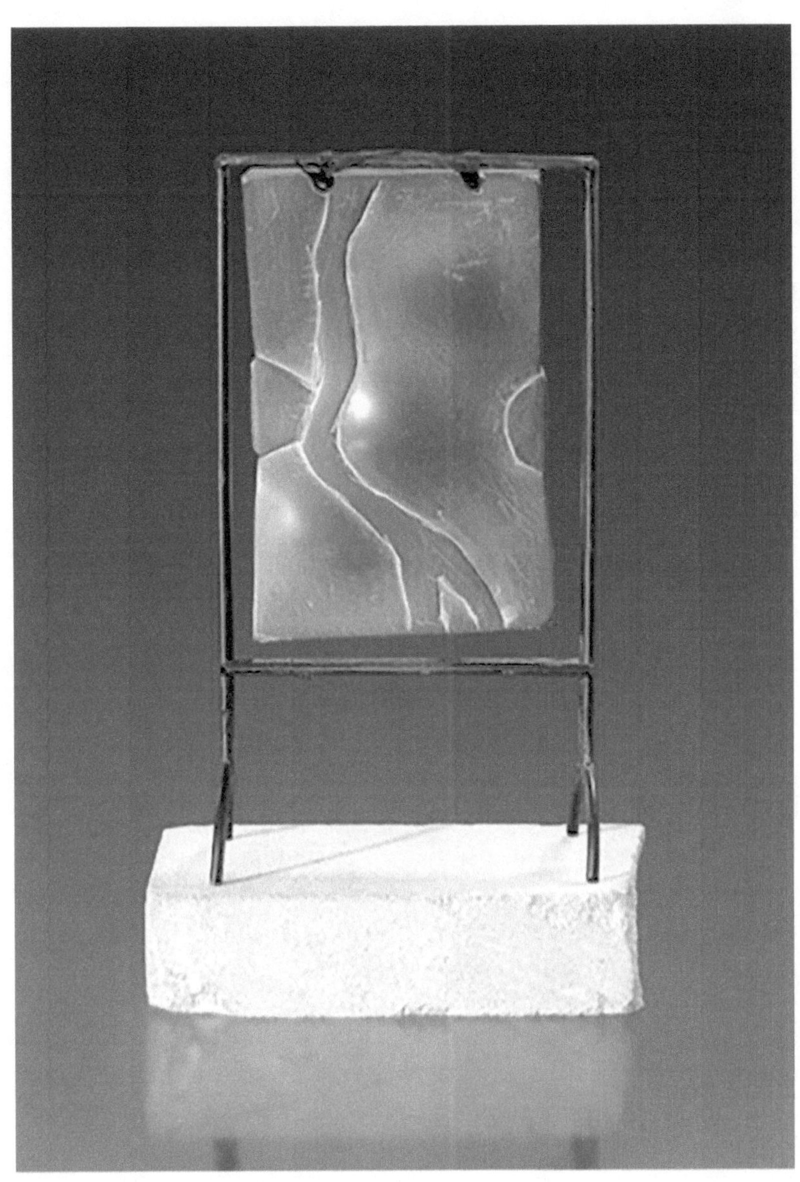

TO CONSTRUCT A SCULPTURE

Where and how does a sculpture begin? How is it formulated in the mind and realized in matter?

Images that motivate the desire for making sculpture may arise from non-visual as well as three-dimensional forms. I believe that these images are developing in the mind even if they remain on the subconscious level and only begin to emerge after the shaping of the material has started. I may approach materials free of associations, or at least make an attempt to do so, but as soon as the shaping starts, past images will enter into the form.

As stated above, these images may have their source in origins other than the visual realm. They may arise from the sound and silence in music, as in Coltrane's complex variations in "Saturn." It may be the smoke rising from the battlefield in Stephen Crane's novel *Red Badge of Courage* or in the sensation of the two sides of an avocado leaf—one side smooth, the other rough. Although one is dealing with sculpture, a visual art, we must develop fully and integrate all our sensibilities. This may be coupled with the visual arts not directly related to sculpture. It can be the party as seen reflected and enlarged through glass in the film *Citizen Kane*, the Open Theatre's *Terminal*, Merce Cunningham's dance or Mark Rothko's colors loaded with mystery.

It's important to base a visual memory on all things recorded by the mind. An interesting experiment is to fill a paper with images based on memory to see how combinations are arrived at and what will be rejected. It can be thought of as learning the English language. As a child, one says "See Spot run." As we use the language our vocabulary grows in order to express all shades of meaning.

Sculpture begins with the self, and all its likes, dislikes, and limitations. A vast interior is within each of us, a universe in completion with some of the stars shining bright, while others are obscured in darkness. If one wants to get to the source, get into your soul, turn on the lights and see everything.

So far, this is still the preparation and not the actual making of sculpture. Ultimately, the sculpture must have its own reason for existing so that references outside of its own formulation cease. The subject will then become the sculpture itself.

What is required in both perceiving and creating sculpture is a balance. To experience sculpture, discovering a little about the artist and focusing a great deal on expanding your vision through the perception of three-dimensional qualities is the synthesis you will want to achieve. The freer the form is from associations, the more it will gain in universality. When the treatment of form is too intellectual, meaning is given to its literary value, and a form is made to mean a specific thing rather than allowing the unconscious to rise up and take form. The beginning of art is not in mental association but rather in the unconscious that has implications for all of us. Most people are only able to project emotion into a figurative statement. However, that is not to imply that non-figurative sculpture is without emotional content.

I have discussed the image. Now I'll proceed to its realization. The idea may be first tested out on a small scale called a *maquette*, or model, a warming-up exercise to discover if the idea is useful to pursue further. It is best done in any material that is inexpensive and in which you can work quickly such as paper, clay, plaster, or cardboard.

If the maquette has the feeling of looking right—which also implies that it may look clumsy or awkward—you can move on to realizing that image on a larger, physical scale. The first decision you have to make is deciding what material you will use for the enlargement, and the second decision concerns the scale you will use for the larger piece. What is the right material for the image, and how large or small should the sculpture be? Dimension is the inner measuring of the form, and scale is the measuring of the sculpture to the world surrounding it.

We usually tend to give sculpture a scale based on our own physical scale in the world. This personal scale may be both physical and psychological. At what level do our eyes look out upon the world and perceive it? We may live in the city surrounded by tall buildings, working in a dark room, lit by unnatural light, or we may be in the country measuring ourselves against mountains, seen through swift-moving clouds that are illuminated by the sharp rays of the sun. Our environment questions us constantly on how we feel about ourselves. Are we large enough to give battle to the elements on equal footing, or are we growing smaller in the darkness of closets? It takes conscious effort to make the sculpture relative to itself. By this I mean seeing the sculpture as an entity, seeking its own scale.

How man perceives himself has changed drastically in the last seventy years. For centuries, man looked out upon the world astride a horse, giving him an elevation of eleven feet. How different the world looked to him than it does to us. Man was closer to the animal world, as together they devoured space. Now we ride through space, sitting capsulized within a machine. Perceiving the world through glass, we are separated from space. From five feet we view the world, which has grown smaller as the horizon has become closer. Our eyes are narrowed to the grey line of concrete that now acts as our guide. We move through space unaware of it, without ceremony.

If we can establish the material and scale, the relationship between gravity and sculpture must next be worked upon. Gravity is a force we contend with every day of our lives. We either succumb to gravity, lying down, or we stand upon the earth. The sculpture must do the same in a dialogue with gravity, as manifested in the ground plan. Will the piece roll with gravity, or defy it? This dialogue is the core of the sculpture, the unseen internal goings-on behind the surface, and is called the axis. Should the axis move horizontally, hugging the ground in a close relationship, or pull away in a vertical position? New England church spires are a good example of the vertical axis, a needle, a point jabbing into space, as if fighting to stay clear of the earth.

A sculpture may have more than one axis, combining vertical and horizontal. If it does, then a balance should be maintained so that an internal conflict isn't set up. A relationship can have contrast, but the sculpture shouldn't have to fight itself. It has enough fighting to do just to maintain a place in the world. It is also possible to push the axis off of the piece, or to the outer limits.

Once the internal ordering is established, the process of external ordering of form is begun. Will the forms be simple or complex? As the viewer's eyes perceive the forms they should be drawn into the piece. If the eye is faced with chaos, it won't be able to differentiate the sculpture from the everyday jumble of surrounding images. If the eye moves too easily through a sculpture, one will not be challenged, and loss of interest will occur. A balance must be maintained so that the eye moves into a piece through a rhythm of forms punctuated by a disruption of unresolved form, while still maintaining a unity.

Once the forms are ordered, the surface must be prepared. How will the forms meet the surrounding space? Will they slide together smoothly, or clash? It is at this stage of development that our tactile, or touch, sense, is brought into the sculpture. Should the sculpture encourage people to touch it, or try to maintain a distance? Touching reinforces the visual memory of a sculpture. How well I remember seeing and touching Michelangelo's *Night*, a reclining figure of a man representing night, found in the Medici Chapel in Florence, Italy. The toe of this sculpture glows from centuries of having been touched.

Finally, the color of the form must be established. Color is now applied to both natural or manufactured material. The artificial coloring of form was questioned until recently. For example, Rodin could never accept the fact that the Greeks painted their marble statues. Today, color on any material is accepted as an integral part of the sculpture.

There are three categories of color: the natural coloring of the material itself, the addition of color, and light falling on the sculpture. The first two categories can be controlled by the sculptor, but the last is usually outside his area of control. Materials usually look better in their natural state, but they can be strengthened at times through the application of color. The color must be integrated with the form and not give a two-dimensional surface to the sculpture, as if it were a skin on the form. Smooth surfaces tend to fuse color into the form more easily than textured surfaces in which the color can act as a concealment to the form.

Color can also help to clarify a combination of forms and to sharpen the imagery. Light, natural or artificial, falling on a piece, can give weight to certain forms, brightening one form and allowing others to recede into shadow. The danger is that the light can become a theatrical device, allowing a two-dimensional silhouette to dominate the forms, rather than three-dimensional qualities.

The sculpture is now completed, ready to leave the studio and meet the world. Is this sculpture an indoor or an outdoor piece? Will it exist on the ground level, eye level, or above? Our eye level states the scale, and we move up or down off of it. If the sculpture is based and artificially placed at eye level with a pedestal, it acts as a barrier to the environment, isolating the piece the same way a frame isolates a painting. The base-pedestal may be integrated into the sculpture, still maintaining its function as support, but may become the focal point of the sculpture.

Tradition has passed down to us this process for the making of sculpture. To take as fact the traditional process is to defeat sculpture. Each sculpture must create its own rules while in the process of being made, and its own theories for existing. It can't be packaged into a set of pre-existing limitations.

Theories, rules, laws, and ideals do not make art. Art comes out of an inner fire. This may drive a person into making mistakes, but we may learn more about ourselves from our mistakes than from our successes.

Sculpture should be a process of crystallization. First there is an idea, the basis of an internal ordering of a structure, expanded or split into different shapes, constantly changing in direction, attracted and repulsed by various forces. The form of the work is the consequence of this interaction. Thus, every new work should be a new crystal, a new being. Like stars in the night sky, each sculpture defined by its own space but interacting with others, making up the fabric of a universe.

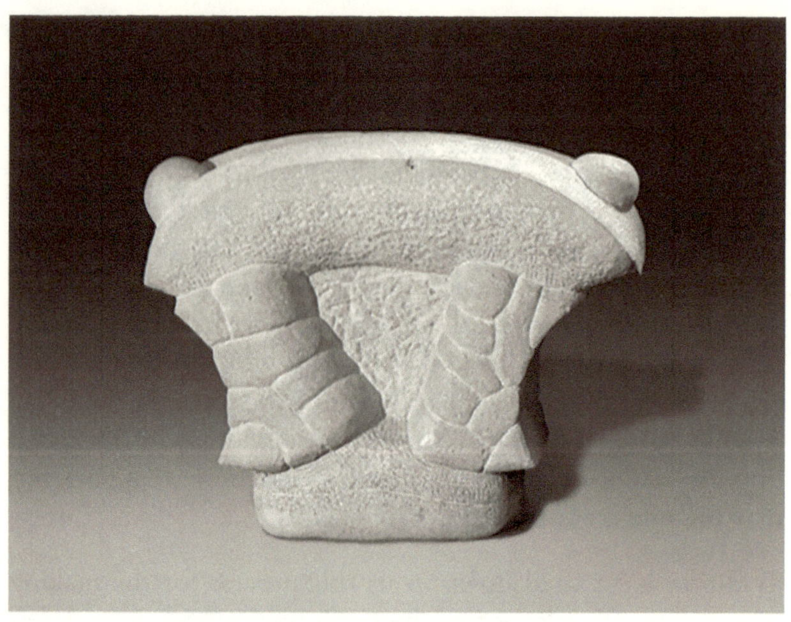

MYTHOLOGY OF STONE

What is stone, that it is so compelling? What is the history of humans and stone? Who are those among us that have particularly informed our understanding of the material I have chosen to spend my life with? The reflections that follow are results of my own musings and perusing; they are a bit like the separate blocks of a sculpture that make up a whole. They are accounts and insights that have resulted from my dialogues with stone.

They begin with four ways of stating our relationship to materials.

The First: All the information of our world is known and defined. We understand this information and can draw conclusions about the world. We can, for example, understand its area: We know that "600 miles deep" is beyond our ability ever to get there:

"The earth is a ball of rock 7927 miles in diameter, weighing about 6.6 trillion tons. It is composed of a dense core as heavy as iron and several massive rock layers denser near the core and lighter towards the surface. The continents themselves are islands of granite rock floating on the denser, darker rocks which underlie the ocean basins and go down perhaps 600 miles" (Zim 7).

The Second: The information of our world can be dissected. As with the first, we can establish an overall view. We can now take a particle, analyze it and find components that are within our own human bodies:

The specific gravity of calcite (CaCO3) is 2.7, and the specific gravity of dolomite is 2.9. Dolomite varieties are thus naturally slightly heavier.

The Third: We deal with the relationship between our self and material in an attempt to understand that relationship rather than any of the material's individual elements:

"Stone comes from the ME Ston. Earlier Stan from OE stara: of OFris and OS sten, OHS-MHG-G stein, GO steins, MD stein, stein, MD-D stein, ON pebble; IE r. *stat-. varr**stei-. *sti - a stone; perhult akin to *sta - to stand" (Partridge 670).

The Fourth: We endeavor to discover the psychological self by way of materials. "Go to a lonely place and rub a stone in a circle on a rock for hours and days on end" (Freuchen 158).

In all four relationships, there is the self and there is the object. In each one, however, we perceive objects differently. The first three ways are modern and very much with US. They are the ways in which we are taught. Materials are known; therefore we can analyze and exploit. We can use them. We can define and take. But we cannot approach and let be. We can bring nature into our world, but we can't enter hers.

The fourth way is one we have lost: the understanding that matter is sacred and can give us knowledge of ourselves. But it is this approach that leads to discovery. We don't know what a stone is or what rubbing a circle will cause—but we do know that it will give birth to something new.

We've defined materials in relationship to ourselves; how would materials define us in relationship to them? How would stone define humans in relationship to itself? Would stone see us as a disturber? Or would stone see us as an extension of itself as we cut, grind, and stack it in our artificial mountains?

We cannot go into the world of stone to answer these questions, and so I will concentrate on stone in our world and on the four ways of relating to it that I have just described. All four are similar in that each is conceived from a human perception and definition. All four are mysterious: I have a vision of myself on the surface of a rock hurtling through space, and I wonder why I am not blown off as I have seen particles of earth fly off a rock I have thrown. Who is going to say which side of earth is down so that we can set the scale underneath that will tell us 6.6 trillion tons? What in the world is CaCO3 and why does that define calcite? It is like entering into the magic squares of Dürer's *Melancholia*; even if I thought I understood Ca, in time it would still prove to be a mystery. Perhaps a linguistic scholar understands **sti - a stone; perhult akin to *sta,* but to me it is in the realm of the unknown.

The fourth, however, is mysterious in a different way. It goes beyond what I do not know into a possibility that something new will be born. Rubbing a stone on a rock for days on end is something I know about. I have polished a piece of stone sculpture. The material is put into motion as part of your body, and together you are part of the motion of a still larger stone, which in turn makes the same motions as it travels through the universe. You become a link in the movement of the universe as it circles through space. You become a part of a mystery. You are within and participating in that mystery, not outside where you can only regard and define it.

This mystery is sacred, and it is by way of this sacred mystery that I explore the mythology of stone. It is sacred because it has the quality or power to reveal the place of humanity in the universe. I am in dialogue with that mystery every time I touch stone; it is perhaps the reason for my choice of stone as a sculptor. And I am not alone in this dialogue. The sacred as expressed in stone has been part of the whole history of humankind. By going into some of that history, I will perhaps discover my own connections with the universe. Perhaps I won't. In any case, I will be faithful to the dialogue with my material.

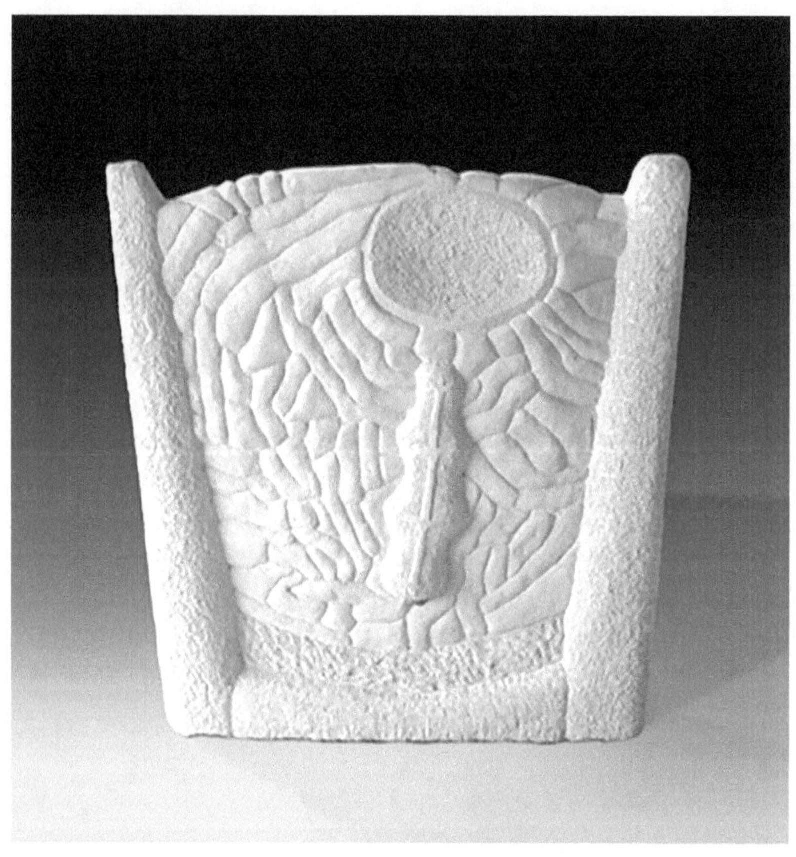

TAKING THE SIDE OF THINGS

The French writer Francis Ponge takes the side of things. Having felt that he couldn't grasp absolute truths in ideas, he opted for objects. The physical forms of materials that we relate to each day could be trusted, he felt, whereas those truths in ideas could be invalidated by contradictory ideas. Because there is no acquired capital, no solid ground to step on or over, ideas remain in a state of flux like the sea, and in Ponge they provoked feelings of nausea.

“However, ideas, opinions, strike me as determined in each of us by something quite different from free will or judgment. I don’t know anything more subjective. I really don’t understand how one can be proud of them, and what I find intolerable is that one tries to impose them on others” (Ponge 81).

In his essay “My Creative Method,” Ponge explains his mistrust of ideas, and then goes on to explain why he has devoted himself to cataloging and defining objects in the external world. He asks himself:

“How is it then that there is more than one dictionary in the same language during the same period, and yet their definitions of the same objects are not identical? How is it that what one finds there seems to be more a definition of words than of things? Why is there this difference between the definition of a word and the description of the thing designated by the word? Why is it that dictionary definitions seem to be so lacking in concreteness and descriptions so incomplete, so arbitrary, so capricious? Couldn’t one imagine some kind of writing which, placing itself more or less between the two (definition and description), would borrow from the former its infallibility; and from the latter its respect for the sensory aspect of things” (Ponge, 83).

In his book *Taking the Side of Things*, Ponge chooses objects, and in writing about them he has been able to let his wing fall between definition and description. There is thus a delight in his writings —a certain joy discovered as he lives and works in this physical world of wonderful objects, objects which exist in themselves and therefore do not ask for human approval of their being.

What Ponge is trying to define is important because he is exploring a major crisis facing our civilization: how we relate to our material world. We have lost touch with objects themselves.

"What is completely spontaneous in man as he touches the earth is an immediate feeling of familiarity, sympathy, or even veneration of matter: Is anything more fitting for the spirit? Whereas spirit venerating spirit ... Can you see that? One sees only too much of it" (Ponge 152).

Our product-oriented society has become interested only in the ends to be gained from products. We exploit the raw materials given to us from the earth and we don't know where to dump the trash we leave behind. Ponge points out that a look at how objects are defined in any dictionary will confirm that the ideas about the objects have become more important than the objects themselves; the abstraction is the important thing. We are drowning in our own creations. William Carlos Williams captures this fact in "Spring and All":

"The pure products of America go crazy ... / As if the earth under our feet were an excrement from the sky."

How can we change this direction? It will happen only if we develop a love for this place called earth. We must change our viewpoint that heaven is someplace else and see it as part of this world, this earth, this place. We must understand our coexistence with the matter we share space with.

Ponge devotes a long section in *Taking the Side of Things* to the pebble. He begins by describing the pebble as a form or state of stone somewhere between rock and gravel. He goes back to the very beginning of time, sees stone as the earth, and follows it as it wears away through natural processes to rock, pebble, gravel, and finally sand. He understands the history of the earth as continual perpetual disintegration. Larger fragments—slabs of stone—nuke the global skeleton, and on them nature germinates, invades, and fractures. It is a natural process of living and dying. Plants linger, fade, and die away; they leave seeds which germinate and continue their attack on stone. In this process Ponge finds a paradox: Life pretends to envy the indestructibility of its setting, but it contributes to the continued disintegration of that setting.

In this duality:
"... it mistakenly believes its foundation may one day fail it, while believing itself to be eternally renewable.... To die and live again, plants, animals, gasses, and liquids move, more or less rapidly. The great wheel of stone seems to us, practically, and even theoretically immobile; we can only imagine a portion of its slowly disintegrating phase. So contrary to popular opinion which makes stone in man's eyes a symbol of durability and impassiveness, one might say that stone, which does not regenerate, is in fact the only thing in nature that constantly dies" (Ponge 73).

Ponge has made an important discovery: All forms of stone, in all their stages, exist simultaneously in the world. No generations, no past, not any person can touch the full potentials of the world as can stone. In the world of stone, there are no conceptions; everything exists.

Ponge ends his contemplations by describing water and stone. Water is the element which has the strongest effect on stone, and it is the most opposite in character. It is liquid; it cannot hold its own form but is a dive to gravity. (We can shape it to our own desires, even lead it through pipes.) It is water that shapes the pebble; but try as it might to penetrate the pebble, water can only wear it away. The pebble may come out smaller as a result of its interaction with water, but it will be intact. However, it does away with the water entirely and with no effort. Once the pebble is removed from the water, the water dries immediately and disappears.

"So that when vanquished, it finally becomes sand. [But] water can still not penetrate it. Keeping all traces except those of liquid, which limits itself to trying to erase all other traces, it lets the whole sea filter through, which disappears into its depth without in any way being able to make mud of it" (Ponge 76).

All of this happens and exists without having anything to do with it. But we do not seem happy with simply understanding and observing the phenomena. We try to enter into it, to bring it into our own realm. We force stones, plants, and animals into our conceptual chaos in order to seek to satisfy our own human pleasures. We do not often wonder about the civilization of the stone until someone like Ponge shares his sensibilities with us and invites us to consider ourselves as part of our world.

"Such is the globe's appearance today. The severed cadaver of the being that was once the world's grandeur now serves merely as a background for the life of millions of beings infinitely smaller and more ephemeral. In places, their crowding is so dense it completely hides the sacred skeleton that was once their sole support" (Ponge 8).

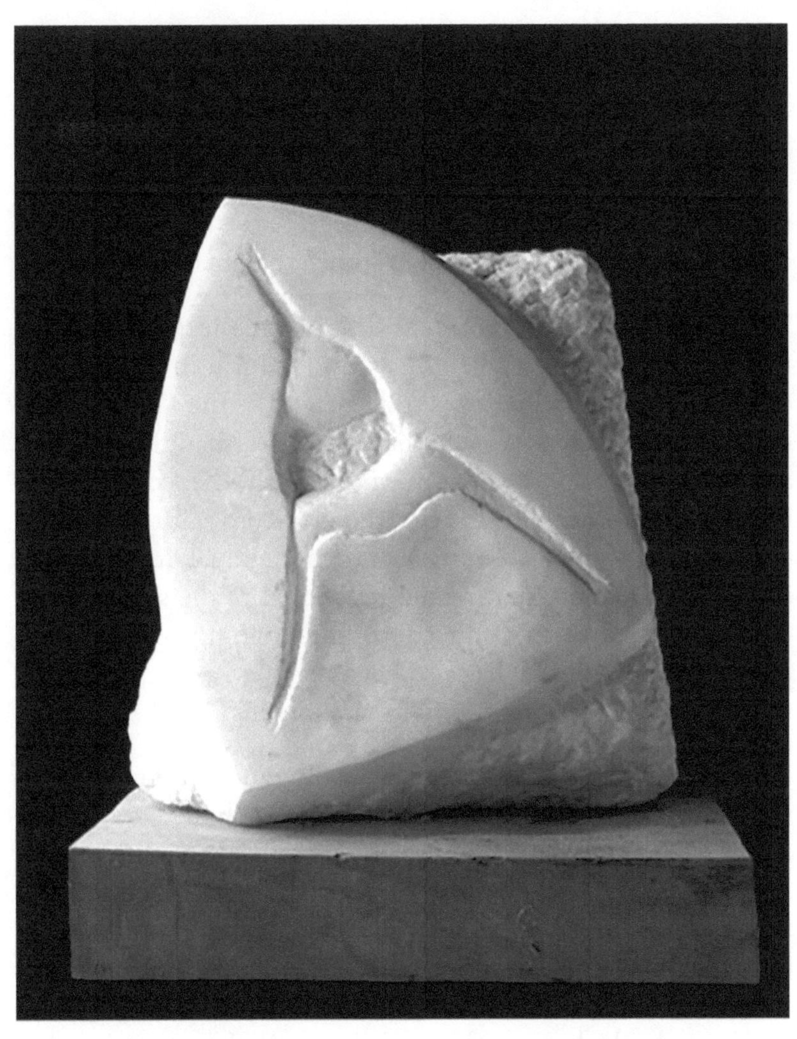

OMPHALOS AND LAPIS MANALIS

There is a stone that links us with the earth and the heavens. It is shaped like a dome and found all over the earth; it is the navel stone, the *omphalos*. Its name is derived from the stone found at the Temple of Apollo at Delphi, Greece. "It is the identification of The Great Earth Mother with stone" (Neumann 260).

The Great Mother is the identification in the psyche of the feminine. It has often taken on symbolic form in the material of stone: in mountains, cases, pillars, rocks. The identification of stone with the navel also has symbolic manifestations; it reminds us of our own connection with the cosmos. The uterus, the mother-body, even the navel-cord, all the symbols of dependency and exist outside of the individual; it is the navel itself which remains part of the individual as the sole mark of this original physical connection and ongoing psychological relationship. The navel has also been regarded as the seat of the soul by reason of its proximity to vital organs.

The omphalos signifies a change in human understanding of the relationship between humans and the earth. It characterized a shift from a celestial geography to a terrestrial one. It became a symbol for the peopling of the land (Rank 192). The omphalos was first seen as the navel of a particular group's homeland: it individualized one's relationship to the earth Later it became abstracted to symbolize the whole earth. As the sacred symbols that brought the heavens down to the earth, the omphalos were located at sites of mountain peaks (Rank 192). The highest points in land elevation became the sacred spots.

In contrast to the layout of the peak-navel, which led to the erection of religious buildings on mountain tops, are the lapis manalis—soul stones. In early city design, the town was built around a center called the mundus. This center was a comblike, circular pit called a *fossa*, the lower part of which was sacred for the spirits of the dead and the gods of the underworld. The pit was closed with a flat round stone called the *lapis manalis* (Rank 192).

We can perhaps interpret the building of towns on the low land as a profane activity; the temple, symbolizing heavenly spiritualism, was erected on the sacred highlands. Maybe we can understand the myth of the building of the Tower of Babel also in light of the sacred/profane duality. Out of the center of commerce an insolent skyscraper was built to reach into the heavens, the most sacred of places, the omphalos.

What does an omphalos look like? The marble omphaloi from Delphi are cone shaped, rounded and not pointed. They are cut from larger blocks and the remaining mass becomes the base, an anchor. They have an erratic snakelike form in relief covering the stone, a navel cord. They may be considered phallic in shape, resembling the lingam in Tantric art; the snakelike projections are seen as similar to the flashes on lingams, the female separating energy. Or they may be thought of as closer in form to the egg. There are lingams in similar egg shape with the snake kundalini coiled about them.

Twentieth-century sculptor Louise Bourgeois makes sculptures based on the same form as the omphalos.

"Sometimes I am totally concerned with the female shapes—cluster of breasts like clouds—but often I merge the imagery—phallic breasts, male and female, active and passive. We are all vulnerable in some way. And we are all male-female" (Bourgeois 56).

The omphalos combines heaven and earth; it also combines the physical and natural worlds. The omphalos is stone.

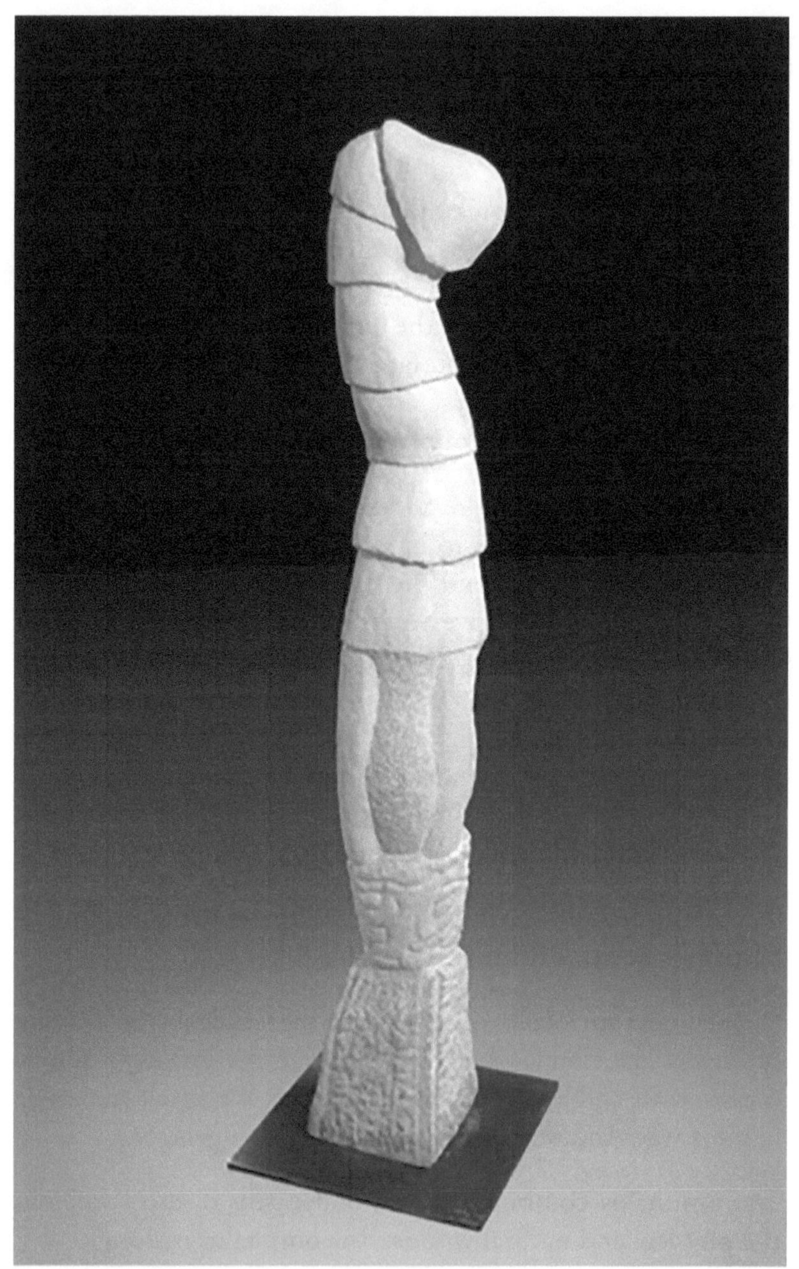

CREATION

Tunkan—the stone God—is the oldest spirit, we think, because he is the hardest. He stands for creation, you know, like the male part. Hard, upright, piercing like the lance and arrow heads fashioned from it in the old days. —Lame Deer

The future doesn't exist, or if it does exist, it is the obsolete in reverse. The future is always going backwards. Our future tends to be prehistoric. —Robert Smithson

Lame Deer explains the role stone plays in the creation of the world. It was there, as it is here today, because it is the most permanent material in nature's world. Robert Smithson observes that how we began seems to be of the utmost importance to us; we yearn our way back to beginnings. His work seems to be a reflection of this yearning. And although his statement on the future tends, on first reading, to sound negative, it is in fact a positive repositioning of man within the realm of nature's process.

"The world was created by God the ruler; he who was hidden within the stone, hidden within the night, was born, where there was neither heaven nor earth. Then he came out of the stone and fell into the second stone. Then it was he declared his divinity" (Roys 111).

Thus begins the creation of the world as found in the book *Chilam Balam of Chumayel.* Although this book was completed in 1782, long after the end of the Mayan civilization, it contains very little European material and is based upon prophecies and history as recounted by Balam, the last and greatest prophet of the Mayan people. Balam lived during the last decades of the fifteenth century, and probably into the beginnings of the sixteenth century. He came into prominence by foretelling the coming of strangers from the East who would establish a new religion. The books were written in the Mayan language, but in European script. They contain chronicles, fragmentary historical narratives, rituals, prophecies, native catechisms, mythological accounts of the creation of the world, almanacs, and medical treatises.

I like Balam's account of the beginning of the world. It begins with God falling between a series of stones. Then "he loosened himself from his stone and declared his divinity" (Roys 111). Why is he created out of a stone? Lame Deer pointed out that stone is the hardest and most durable of materials. This North American Indian called the stone god Tunkan, a name that has its beginnings with the Mayans. The Mayan word for a precious stone is "tun"; the word for an ordinary stone is "tunich." *Tun* is also a term used in the measuring of time; it equaled 365 days. Balam tells us that God was hidden within the stone "where there was neither time nor space" (Roys). The key word is "where"; "when" is not spoken of. Thus the creation is placed beyond time. For the Mayans, the "first time" was outside material creation, so that God had to descend to the "second time" before he could declare his divinity. Is the reference to stone (*tun*), to time (*tun*), or to both?

God continued creating the heavens and earth from stones. Hebones, the only son of God, was born upon the stone of his father; man was born of stone when moisture fell upon it. It is interesting that God, at the first heaven, has a stone in one hand and in the other his kabahil, the Mayan potter's wheel. On the potter's wheel were "hung the four changing winds" (Roys 111), and the stone was used to create the planets "which he held in his grasp when he created them" (Roys 111).

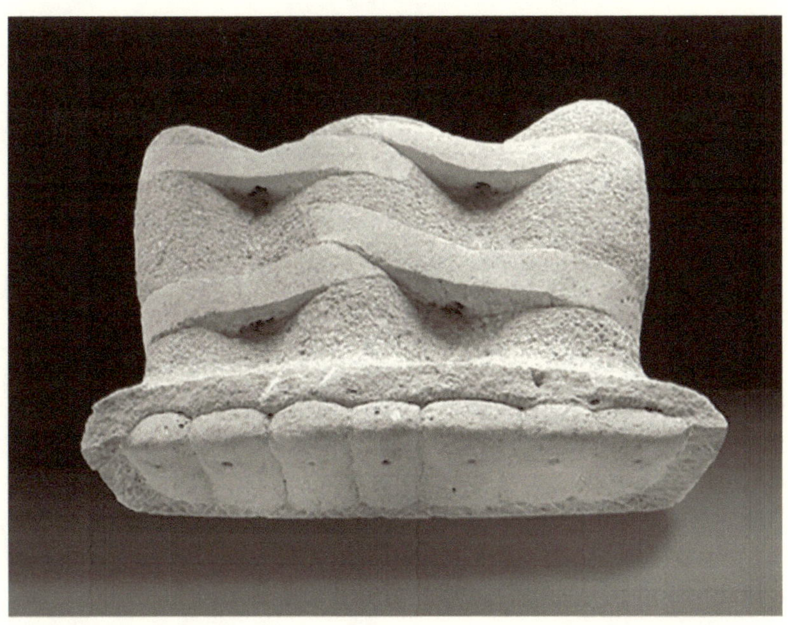

ENGLAND

England and stone—I've always thought of them together. Perhaps one reason for this association is that the British Isles themselves are stones rising out of water. To be in England is to feel the stones beneath one's feet and to be aware of the water not far off.

England and stone—the relationship here is a healthy one. Whatever has been done with stone has been inquisitive and has grown out of a spiritual connection with the earth and the earth's larger home, the universe. In England, there was no impulse to alter stone into a human image, no need to box physical bodies in pyramids as the Egyptians did, no cutting of stones into narcissistic images to grace temples as the Greeks did. In England stone was left free-standing in nature's elements; it conveyed extending forms into space beyond human dimensions and imagery. There is in England no St. Peter's with its round of stone popes, no giant statues of pharaohs long lost in the sand; there is only and always simple undressed stone. Even in Westminster Abbey, the coronation stone was meant to confer wisdom on kings but was never used by kings as an emblem of their power. The king was nothing compared to the stone.

Earthworks, standing stones and circles of prehistory, archaic carvings, ancient buildings and other stone structures, hill figures, mazes, trackways and leys—all of these are found in England. And yet, according to a psychometrist in the presence of stone, "the stone is quite impersonal. I can get no history from it. It has no power to absorb earth radiations ... is in a constant state of transmission of cosmic energy" (Bord and Bord 31).

The earthworks are huge mounds of earth constructed to alter or enhance the currents of natural energies that flowed through the body of the earth, according to one theory. The largest mood in Europe is in England. Called Silbury, it is 130 feet high and covers 5 1/4 acres. Its purpose remains a mystery, but a recent investigation has found that it contains small groups of up to four stones each.

The most impressive standing stones and circles are Stonehenge and Avebury. Both are thought to be solar and moon temples whose design was predicated on the movements of the heavenly bodies. Many individual standing stones exist, and some are situated within a complex of earth works. Some were carried to a sacred location and others were left where nature had brought them. All of them have been given some unique shape by nature. The crosses differ from standing stones in that humans gave them their form, although some were left close to their natural shape. Many individual standing stones were covered with petroglyphs. The earliest chippings on the surface show only symbols; later, letters and words appear. Nothing is known of the meanings of the early "cup and ring" symbols though they have been associated with stars due to their nebula formations and the optical impressions that thereby happen.

There can still be found in England ancient stone buildings that were either underground chambers, called *weems* or round towers, called *brochs*. The underground chambers are thought to be rooms where the earth's energies were focused, benefiting the occupants. Less is known about the round tossers, but it may be that they, too, acted as a magnifier of the earth's energy.

The hill figures found on slopes in England were cut into the soft stone chalk. Some were recleaned over the years while others have been allowed to become overgrown. The Uffington white horse, one of the most well-known, measures 360 feet wide, and the best vantage point for viewing is from the air. What purpose the hill figures were meant to serve is still a mystery. Perhaps they were simply land markings; perhaps they were related to worship of the sun.

At one point, mazes were found all over Britain, but most have now disappeared, having been plowed over. One maze, however, constructed of small stones, still exists. It is named Camperdizil Point, which can be translated at sunrise motion and which may denote a connection with sun worship.

One of the strangest uses of stones has been as markers for what are called *leys*. If you take any survey map of Britain and circle sacred locations such as standing stones, earth works, churches, and other sacred sites, you will find you can run straight lines through the circles; they will align. These alignments are thought by some to be a notation of the earth's energy moving across the land.

In books such as *Mysterious Britain,* these various uses of stone have been well described and detailed. What I wonder as I contemplate the stone uses and sites relates to the overall fabric. What purposes did all of these stone arrangements serve? I don't know, and I marvel at their existence and wonder at their uses. I feel that they connote peacefulness and a respect for the earth and her materials.

Why are these various uses of stone so numerous in and seemingly unique to the British Isles? Perhaps it is only that they are better preserved there. England, unlike most other countries, has suffered little from invading forces. If Egypt hadn't been centered on the crossroads of Asia and Africa, would it have told more of its relationship to stone? If the Incas had not been destroyed by the Spanish, would more have been found there? There are no answers to those questions. What is known is that in England many sites attest to the human connection felt with stones. The mysteries of the connections challenge our thoughtfulness but not our fears. They seem to speak to our spirit.

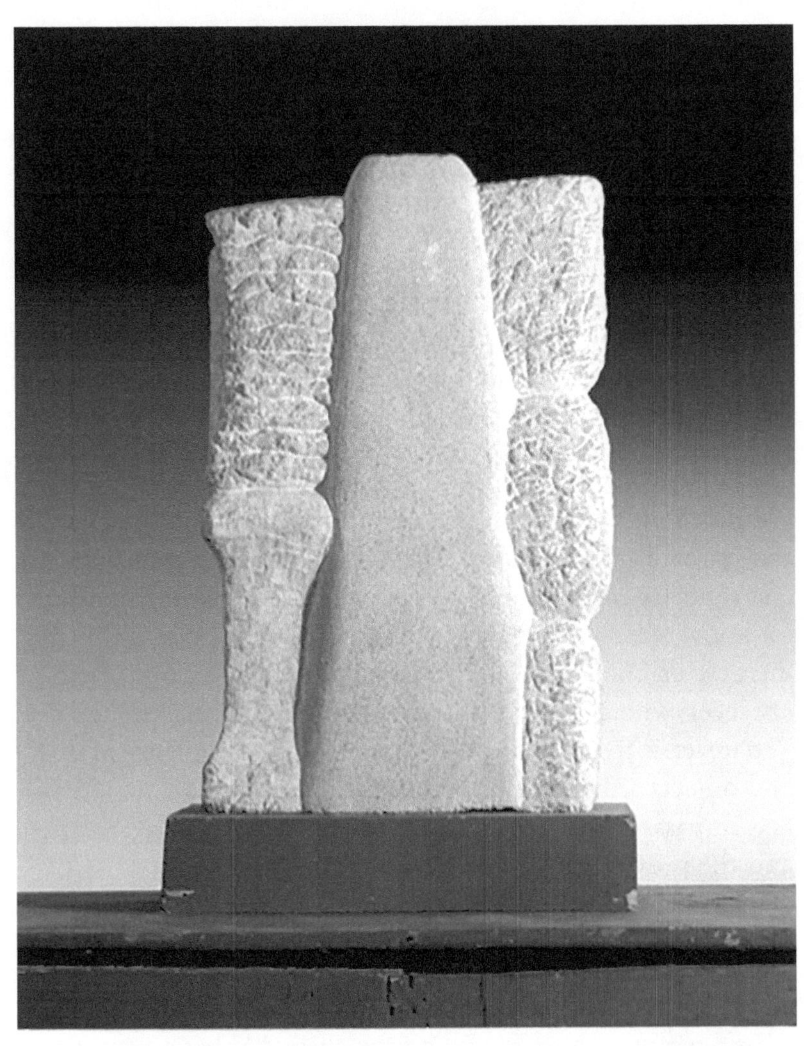

THE STONES OF CAMUS

"*Innocence needs sand and stones. And man has forgotten how to live with them.* —Albert Camus, "The Minotaur"

In Albert Camus' essay "The Minotaur," the stone is king. Set under the strong baking action of the North African sun where nature refuses to let things grow, the essay is about the human fight to survive, to exist. The battle is waged against stones. In Camus' North Africa, the world does indeed seem to be "a large ball of rock," an unchanging and unnatural home for people.

Oran is a city poised on the edge of land; in one direction is the sea, and in the other are the stones of the desert. Both sea and sand are capable of smothering a human. "It is impossible to know what stone is without coming to Oran. In that dustiest of cities, the pebble is king" (Camus 165). Pebbles are everywhere, brought in with the dust of the desert. Whatever is living is soon almost petrified by a layer of dust, and objects are seen through a dusty film that creates a dense and impassable universe. The dust and stones destroy the past and the present cannot be seen.

The minotaur of the essay's title enters the city as boredom. The capital (Oran) of boredom is surrounded by an army in which every stone is a soldier. In the city, and at certain hours, however, what a temptation to go over to the enemy! What a temptation to identify oneself with those stones, to melt into that burning and impassive universe that defies history and its ferments. This is doubtless futile. But there is in every man a profound instinct which is neither that of destruction nor that of creation. It is merely a matter of resembling nothing.

Boredom has entered as the stone, as the unfeeling, mute stone that will not undergo any change. Man loses a sense of his own existence, and inactivity sets in. This inactivity of nothingness must be understood, and after that awareness can come into being. The sun will someday crack the stone; a seed blown by the wind will be caught in the crack; life will begin again. Life will cause changes, and for Camus the answer is to accept both states as one—to know both sleep and wakefulness as parts of the same whole. "If stone can do no more for us than the human heart, it can do just as much" (Camus 181).

For the people of Oran, this awareness takes the form of a frontal attack on the stone. They create a stone jetty that pushes its way out into the sea. The people attack the mountains with dynamite and they transport the loosened rubble to the sea and dump it. And all the while this work is going on. The wind is continuing to dump its own piles of stones and pebbles on the city. "Destroying stone is not possible. It is merely moved from one place to another" (Camus 177). While the people of the city move stone from one location to a different one, nature moves stone into the void that they have created. "The whole city has solidified in a stone matrix" (Camus 165). In this activity, humans will never triumph, and their actions will soon cease to have any meaning; when tomorrow comes they will start all over again, even as nature in the form of wind deposits more stone on the land and in the form of sea wears down the stones on the jetty. Caught in this hopeless round of activity, each person must make a choice: one can continue, or one can stop. For Camus, the important thing is to find meaning in the desire to persevere.

Camus writes harshly on the stones that define this activity, but he also writes on the beauty to be found in nature. He finds that beauty in the stones of a beach near Oran and in the stones found in the solitude of deserts far from Oran. Living with both the beauty and the struggle is part of the innocence that Camus knows we need. But he recognizes that we too often only interpret stone in the context of our own point of view in relationship to the struggle. Stones would do very well without us, but could we survive without stone? If we had no stones, would we have to invent them to define our own activities? We have a choice. We can lose ourselves in the harshness or in the beauty of this world, or we can embrace that harsh beauty and work with it.

"It is noon; the very day is being weighed in the balance. His rite accomplished, the traveler receives the reward of his liberation: the little stone, dry and smooth as an asphodel, that he picks up on the cliff. For the initiate the world is no heavier to bear than this stone. Atlas's task is easy; it is sufficient to choose one's hour. Then one realizes that for an hour, a month, a year, these shores can indulge in freedom" (Camus 182).

A face that toils so close to stone is already stone itself —Albert Camus

Camus' imagery based on stone is nowhere more profound than in his description of Sisyphus, a character with whom I feel a great deal of identification. Working each day with stone, I wonder where all this labor is taking me. I finish one piece, turn, and begin the next, hoping that this will be the time I will state all that I have to say about sculpture. Camus is interested in that moment of turning as he describes Sisyphus' pause on the descent of the hill before he returns again to his labors. There is the moment of awareness, of tragedy and joy, or happiness and the absurd. To understand this moment, you must also know its opposite, for it is out of their intersection and the struggle to embrace them both that you find freedom.

"When the images of earth cling too tightly to memory, when the call of happiness becomes too insistent, it happens that melancholy rises in man's heart; this is the rock's victory, that is the rock itself. The boundless grief is too heavy to bear. But crushing truths perish from being acknowledged" (Camus 122).

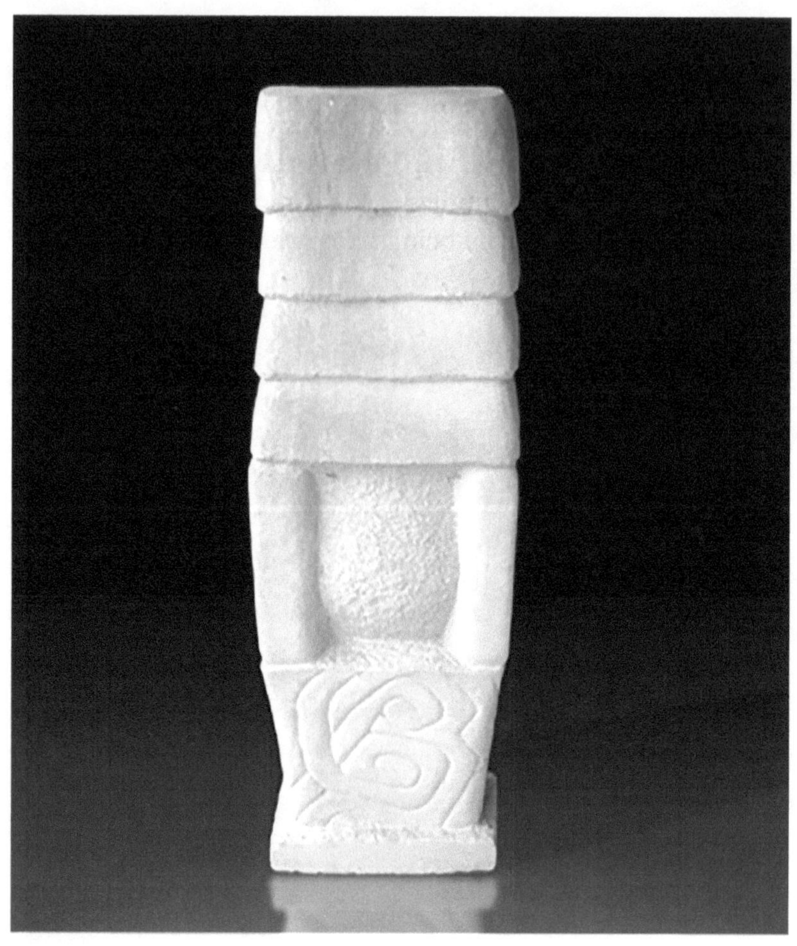

TWENTIETH-CENTURY STONE SCULPTURE

A few blocks of stone really carved are very nearly sufficient base for a new civilization. The garbage of three empires collapsed over Gaudier's marble. —Ezra Pound, *Gaudier-Brzeska*

Thus Ezra Pound described his friend, the sculptor Henri Gaudier-Brzeska. Despite having died in the First World War at the age of twenty-three, Gaudier built the concept of modern sculpture with his stones. How was he able to do this?

He freed the stone from its chains to the imagery of man and returned it to its own self-imagery. He was, in fact, groping his way back to Stonehenge. About his formation of the sculpture called "Vortex," he wrote:

"The fair Greek saw himself only. He petrified his own semblance. His sculpture was derivative, his feeling for form secondary. The absence of direct energy lasted for a thousand years ... [But] we have crystallized the sphere into the cube, we have made a combination of all possible shaped masses concentrating in them our abstract thoughts" (Pound 10).

I have chosen stone for the same reasons Gaudier did. It has the paradox of being both old and new at the same time. I'm doing the same work that has been done for thousands of years but which has been lost for the past five hundred years. Pound described what I believe:

"[Form is] an arrangement of masses in relation. It is not an empty copy of empty Roman allegories that are themselves copies of copies. It is not a mimicry of external life It is the energy cut into stones, making the stone expressive in its fit and particular manner. It has regard to the stone" (Pound 130).

"Stone is hard and concentrated and should not be falsified to look like flesh—it should not be forced beyond its constructive build to a point of weakness, it should keep its hard tense stoniness" (Moore, "Statement," 29).

These ideas about "truth to materials" were familiar concepts to the sculptor Henry Moore. Around 1928 Moore began to make a habit of examining and collecting pebbles. In 1932 he used a pebble, one with a hole through it, as a beginning for a sculpture. In 1934 he made small biomorphic sculptures, like from forms found in nature, by working on found pebbles. He did not do much more than modify the pebble's shape; it is impossible to judge from the finished sculpture what of the form was found and what was imposed. He carved a hole through a pebble in one case, but the hole might equally well have been present in the pebble when he found it. "Pebbles and rocks show nature's way of working stone. Smooth, sea-worn pebbles show that wearing assay, tubbed, treatment of stone and principles of asymmetry" (ibid.).

After 1934, Moore's stone carvings still generally reflect the study of "smooth, sea-worn pebbles," but they begin to differ from those which actually began as pebbles by having a sharp edge somewhere to contrast with the smoothly modulated curves that might have been shaped by the sea. From 1936, the sharp edges multiplied: the carving became more angular than curvilinear. "Rocks show the hacked, hewn treatment of stones and have a "jagged, nervous block rhythm" (ibid.). At that time, Moore made only one small piece with this "jagged, nervous block rhythm," but from 1959 onwards, in his series of two-piece reclining figures, he made much of the idea of imitating rocks.

Clearly Moore's starting point with stone was the same as Gaudier's: both went back to the early human concept of the sacred in stone. Sculpture can be either a sacred object or a mere knick-knack. The primitive belief that material objects are inhabited by spirits is implicit in the doctrine of being true to the essence of the material. "One of the first principles of art so clearly seen in primitive work is truth to material; the artist shows an instinctive understanding of his material, its right use and possibilities" (Moore, *Writings*, 104).

Nevertheless, Moore affirmed the artistic sensibilities necessary to shape the materials: "Otherwise a snowman nude by a child would have to be praised at the expense of a Rodin or a Bernini" (qtd. in Sylvester 4). And when Moore did choose to make his "rock-like sculpture," he chose not stone but a more tractable material, plaster: a soft, molding material he wanted to render as hard!

Moore's work fluctuated between abstractionism and representation. He often stated that abstraction was a flight from reality; maybe he wanted to reassure himself that his work wasn't an escape and that is why he became preoccupied with natural objects. He wanted his sculpture to look organic and hard. He wanted it to evoke images other than themselves. He wanted the shapes that his sculptures were derived from to maintain their mysterious ambiguity. Perhaps Moore's convictions about the value of natural objects were enhanced by an equally strong belief that his abstract forms were obeying some authority beyond that of his own creativity, that they were therefore not arbitrary, not products of mere personal taste or fantasy; he saw them as sanctioned by nature and not simply as representations of his own preferences, his own decisions, his own way of working stone.

"These abstract carvings have not really satisfied me because I have not had the same hold over them that I have as soon as a thing takes on a kind of organic idea. I think of it as having a head, body, limbs; as the piece of stone I carved evolves from the first rounding-out stages, it begins to take on a definite human personality and character" (Moore, *Writings*, 126).

Henry Moore's musings make me turn to my own questioning of why I work in stone. I think it has a lot to do with ability and ease. The technique of stone carving came easily to me from the first stroke of the hammer on a chisel; I felt satisfaction from the sound of the ping that the stone made upon being struck. I felt as if I had always done such things, as if I had been born with hammer and point. I knew the technique and path my mind took, a path often dictated by the feel of the stone. I love the activity of cutting.

I have worked on all varieties of stones and responded to the differences each stone asked for in the way of treatment. But now I no longer work in all stones; I have chosen to express myself in limestone. Its natural gray color does not interfere with the forms. Often a pretty stone such as marble covers up bad forms because people don't really look at the forms that respond to the veining of the crystals in the stone. Limestone, a rough, ragged stone, bears traces of the sea: sea animals are locked into and within the crystal structure. Limestone is American. The hills I was born in are made of this material, and it gives me pleasure to work in Texas limestone. It's friendly, and it reminds me of my roots. Limestone has good tensile strength, allowing thin slab forms to be cut. It has the strength as well to withstand the noxious air of an urban city.

The dead weight of stone allows a sculptor to do incredible balancing acts. If the center of a balanced piece of stone is found, the stone can be suspended in the air; the straight drop of dead weight allows this. And if a stone is put out of balance, it will not slip and fall sideways, since the weight can't fall in a sideways direction.

My ideas on stone have moved towards concerns with structure. I have great freedom in working with this material. I begin the construction in full three-dimensional forms; I allow multiple curves on each individual form; I then group them into a more complex arrangement. Sidney Geist, in his book on Brancusi—one of the finest books ever written on sculpture—sums up in a beautiful way the personal experience of working with stone.

"Sculpture should declare its difference from other objects, and offset the possibility of mistake as to its identity. It should recall the possibility of being used in some fashion or of being grasped like an object of use. It should demand and deserve special attention. And it should be made as to maintain itself in the world and its pristine state. In respect to this last condition, it is helpful for sculpture not to have large horizontal surfaces or such concavities as will invite or accept other objects or hold snow. rain, or dust. To the extent that sculpture is deformed or invaded by nature, it belongs to nature. Brancusian form is freed from nature. It is form seen by the light of human intelligence" (Geist 157).

I am searching constantly for my own direction. Understanding Brancusi's freedom from nature—and Moore and Smithson's re-sinking into nature—are ways to reflect on my own ongoing dialogue with stone.

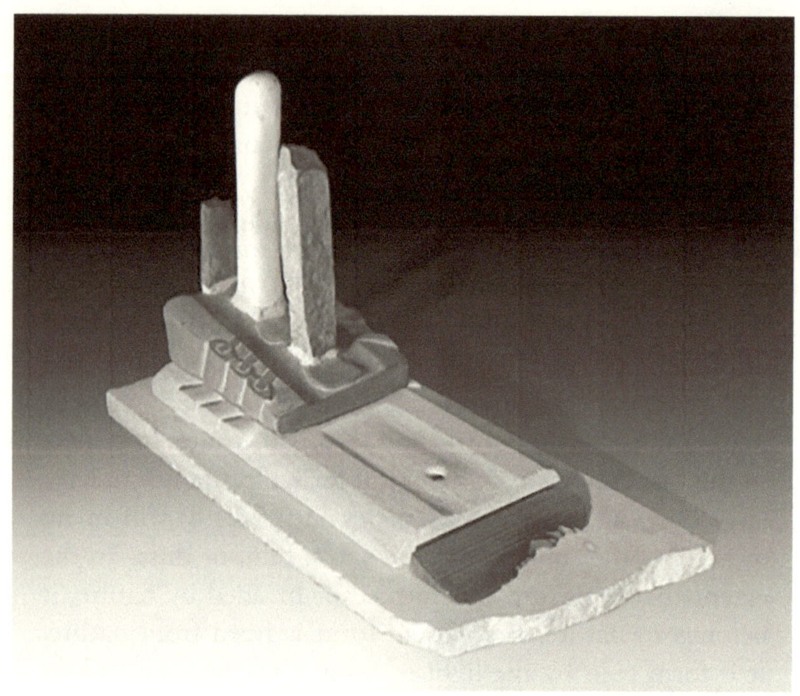

RICHARDSON'S ORIGINAL MONSTER ROCK BAND

So you think that rock music was something new under the sun? Well, the title of this section is from a public handbill printed in 1840. The Richardson family had built a rock xylophone. After thirteen years of cutting and fitting together, they had an incredible instrument that covered seven octaves. The materials came from the Skiddaw mountains in the Lake Region of England; the stones were rendered musical because of a freak of nature: an active volcano in Skiddaw overflowed and the lava, unable to flow out evenly all around because of other close mountains, became compressed in a very small area. A second instrument was made in 1881. It toured the United

States and is now housed in the Museum of Orange, New Jersey. Today these stones are rare, particularly those with deep tones, so it is improbable that another xylophone could be cut.

Stones have been important in other musical traditions as well. There is a Chinese tradition which claims that about 2000 years ago a complete stone chime was found in a pool. This discovery became a model for future instruments. Another legend dates stone chimes back even further, to about 2300 BCE. From this time we have a chant that refers to a musical stone:

"When I smite my musical stone—be it gently or strong Then do the fiercest hearts leap for joy

And the chiefs do agree among themselves. When ye make to resound the stone melodious.

When ye touch the lyre that is called Ch'in,

Then do the ghosts of the ancestors come to hear" (Blades 91).

In Confucian music, the stone was struck to end a verse and to transmit the tone to the next verse.

The materials of the instruments in a Chinese orchestra were believed to express the changes and permutations taking place in the universe. The sonorous stone was charted thusly:

Cardinal Point Season Phenomena Substance—Northwest Autumn, Winter Heaven Stone

Lithophones have been found elsewhere in the world: in Ethiopia, Nigeria, in Venezuela, and in Europe on the islands of Chios and Sardinia. In southern India there are musical stone pillars: there are the Ye stones of the Central Highlands of West

New Guinea. In West Polynesia, there is a rite used to prepare the intoxicating drink Kawa for religious purposes: maidens perform the solemn ceremony of sitting on the ground and pulverizing the roots of a pepper plant on flat sonorous stones; these stones are insulated with small pieces of coconut and tuned to definite pitches. Laura Bolton in her book *The Music Hunter* describes two lithophones found in 1950 in what is now central Vietnam. Made by the Bacsonians, a tropical race of Stone Age men that thus perhaps date the instruments as far back as 9000 years, they may turn out to be the oldest known musical instruments in the world.

The Rolling Stones have been with us a long time!

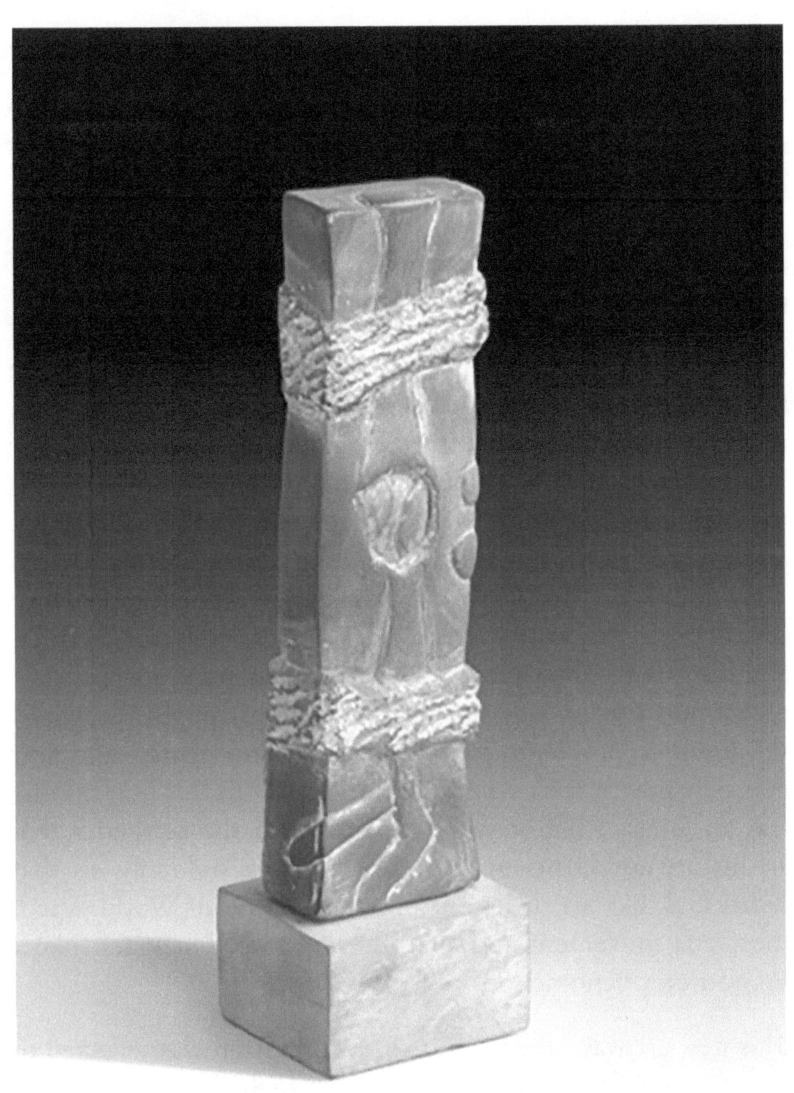

ROBERT SMITHSON

"My work is impure; it is filled with matter. I'm for a weighty ponderous art. There is no escape from the matter. There is no escape from the physical nor is there any escape from the mind. The two are in a constant collision course. You might say that my work is like an artistic disaster. It is a quiet catastrophe of mind and matter" (Smithson qd. in Lippard 89).

By the mid-1960s, the anti-war movement had begun to be felt throughout all facets of American society. It affected the artist as well as his society. But artists' statements didn't become politicized in the same way the muralists did during the Mexican Revolution. Rather, they questioned social roles, and the way artists handled their work in a consuming society. They questioned art objects for sale in a market equipped with distributors, magazines, dealers, museums, collectors, critics, and historians. They questioned three thousand years of the art object and how it was put to use by kings, popes, burghers, social causes, problems, greeting cards, governments—and now that new power, the corporation. The result of this questioning was an art that had very little to do with the aesthetics that art history and criticism studied. There was, suddenly, art that didn't look like art. It had its roots in the end of World War I, the Dada movement and Marcel Duchamp, but it felt like a brand-new phenomenon.

This new art was called Minimal. Its intention was reflected in its name; the form was reduced until it reached a point where it just didn't look like sculpture or painting. As interest in the art object lessened there developed new interest in the process of making, in the artists' perceptions and plans, and even the artist. Gone was interest in the art object—which had indeed ceased to be an “object.” As usual, however, everyone underestimated the flexibility of the art market and its long tradition; our society seems well able to incorporate any protest. Minimalism became an art movement and attached itself with ease to the three thousand years of Occidental art.

One of those artists who questioned and continued to pursue new directions was Robert Smithson. He was seen to be working in new ways but actually his earthworks seem to predate all out concepts of Western art. Rather than abstracting concepts and materials, his work was done in natural environments and was involved with geological changes. Smithson embraced his own destiny; he embodied all the contradictions and confusions of our society; he created a body of work that expressed innocence.

“Actually, it is the mistakes we make that result in something. There is no point in trying to come up with the right answer because it is inevitably wrong. An art against itself is a good possibility, an art that always returns to essential contradictions. I’m sick of positivists, ontological hopes, and that sort of thing, even ontological despairs. Both are impossible” (qtd. in Lippard 89).

Robert Smithson’s long walk began in 1966 with a piece called *Tar Pool and Gravel Pit.* It had reference to the tar pits of California where skeletal remains of dinosaurs were found. In this work, geological processes were the subject: What happens when tar cools and flattens into a sticky deposit? The *Tar Pool* was shown in a gallery, isolated from real geological processes. Out of it grew the concept of “non-sites,” given the neutral environment of the gallery. That quality of neutrality was explored in a variety of ways. Sometimes the insertion of mirrors resulted in material that became pure illusion.

Another aspect of non-site work used maps as a substitution for materials. They were cut up, repositioned and overlapped; they became his most "finished" works. If you have a love of maps as I do, finding magic in them, you can't help but be awakened to new ways of reviewing a map by the way Smithson has made perspectives push, recede, and blend into each other.

In 1966 Smithson was a consultant for an architectural-engineering firm that was competing for the design of the Dallas/Fort Worth Airport. The project would have allowed Smithson to realize his work outside of the art world. It did not materialize, but it was a catalyst for Smithson to begin to explore other possibilities. From it came the concept of "site work"—work that would have its place in its natural setting. Smithson listed some variables between "site" and "non-site":

SITE:

1. open limits
2. series of points
3. outer coordinates
4. subtraction
5. indeterminate certainty
6. scattered information
7. reflection
8. edge
9. someplace (physical)
10. many

NON-SITE:

1. closed limits
2. an array of matter inner coordinates addition
3. determinate certainty contained information mirror
4. center
5. no place (abstraction) one

(Smithson, "Dialectic")

Smithson chose for his first site work the Yucatan, and he brought to it an element from his non-site work—it involved the placement of mirrors. "Reflections fall into mirrors without logic and in so doing invalidate every rational assertion" (Smithson, "Incidents"). This was the only time Smithson used mirrors in site work, although he continued to use them in non-site work.

That same year 1969, Smithson worked on his first earthwork free of artificial qualities. The *Asphalt Rundown* involved the flow and displacement of material: Asphalt was poured from a truck and allowed to run down an incline. Judging from the color photos, the resulting color combinations were exceptional. Perhaps Smithson had in mind an observation he had made in 1966: "instead of using a paintbrush to make his art, Robert Morris would like to use a bulldozer" (Smithson, "Towards"). The dump truck had become the paintbrush, and the pigment cascaded down the "canvas"—it was a very painterly earthwork.

Partially Buried Woodshed, in 1970, continued his interest in the flowing principle. It was a work pure in intent. There were no mirrors and no aesthetics, nothing but the force of nature. Earth was allowed to accumulate around and on top of a wood shed until the roof beam broke. At that point the work ended. "The slow flowage makes one conscious of the turbidity of thinking. Slump, debris slides, avalanches, all take place within the cracking limits of the brain" (Smithson qtd. in Lippard 56).

The *Spiral Jetty* that Smithson built in 1970 in the Great Salt Lake is his best-known work. Composed of a spiral starting on the edge of the lake and spiraling out counterclockwise into the lake, it exists on many levels, both visual and psychological; it remains open to all interpretations. The lake was chosen because of its physical properties, notably a high density of salt that gives it a reddish color and which crystallizes on its border and thus on the work itself. The color of the water changes as it moves into the spiral, and the rocks composing the spiral change colors as well. It might also have been chosen because of legends about it, that it was once part of an ocean and contained whirlpools. The spiral form itself is a mystery containing no past, present, or future; it escapes all systems of thought, aesthetics, history, and philosophy.

A pair of earthworks in Holland stand as a unit. *Broken Circle and Spiral Hill,* 1971, involves opposites. The broken circle is connected to earth and water, while the spiral hill equals earth and air. The broken circle lies flat on the horizon while the spiral is on an incline.

Smithson did not live to see the completion of his last work, *Amarillo Ramp*. The plane he was in for the purpose of mapping the work from the air stalled and crashed, killing all aboard. The work was completed by his wife, Nancy Holt, and his close friends Richard Serra and Tony Shafrazi. People have questioned whether or not it can rightfully be called Smithson's work. But all three who completed it had been involved with Smithson during the planning stages; they understood his work and what he wanted to achieve. The fact that Smithson also liked to allow chance to play a part in his work, and that he was always open to suggestions and changes, argues for the *Amarillo Ramp* in his oeuvre. The ramp is sited on a private ranch in the panhandle region of Texas, and it is composed of rocks which are in sharp contrast to the lake and surrounding desert. The lake it sits upon is man-made for the purposes of irrigation; consequently the water level changes and affects the slant of the ramp as it cuts across the low, flat horizon.

"As long as art is thought of as creation it will be the same old study. Here we go again, creating objects, creating systems, building a better tomorrow. I posit that there is no tomorrow, nothing but a gap, a yawning gap. That seems sort of tragic, but what immediately relieves it is irony. It is that cosmic sense of humor that makes it all tolerable. Everything just vanishes. The sites are receding into non-sites, and the non-sites are receding back to the sites, it is always back and forth, to and fro. Discovering places for the first time, then not knowing them" (Smithson qtd. in Lippard 90).

Why is Robert Smithson so important? I can only answer for myself. Stones, contradictions, and an ability to maintain humor through it all are the essentials of his work. He had a love of stones in all their multi-textures, colors, and forms. He knew them well, how they change and how minerals can work on them. I share that love, but I'm also a robber of stones - cutting, banging, stacking, pushing them to their breaking point. I put them in unnatural settings. Smithson allowed them to continue the natural process of change; I try to arrest them, to fix them down and at the same time to free them from their environment.

Smithson lived the social and artistic contradictions we are all faced with. All his works are open; none are based on any closed system of thought. His minimal work—in contrast to other minimalists—was based on geometric forms that could either expand or contract. When he resorted to mirrors, it was to enhance that openness. He maintained this vision in the earthworks, and it was a vision that communicated to others.

The operator of the front-end loader at the *Amarillo Ramp,* a man who had worked his whole life doing construction jobs, said that this project "was like going into outer space. You're going up all the time and just come to an end there, where you don't know where you go from there" (Holt 20).

Smithson also faced the contradictions inherent in his acceptance of both site and non-site situations. He could abstract material-neutral environments, and even the most artificial rooms that do not ordinarily partake of life: museums and galleries. Later he substituted the photographic image for materials - all the while admitting that photographs steal away the spirit of the work. He created the most public art, and yet it is the least accessible to the public because of its locations.

His humor allowed him to envision a nature tableau being pulled around Manhattan by a tugboat. He could wed the image of rotting bananas with the music of Captain Beefheart's "I love you, ya big dummy." Upside-down trees in Florida? He could live with it all. Smithson accepted the build-up and decay of matter, the natural and the unnatural. He knew that progress increases waste and that his own work would fall apart. He put his ideas, opinions, and dreams into an art that was free of ego. Ultimately, for us, he made it possible to walk into the Spiral Jetty. It's a walk that Smithson made difficult, for we can spiral into ourselves, or we can turn around and walk against the clock, out into the universe.

"All those guide books are of no use.
You must travel at random, like the first Mayans.

You risk getting lost in the thickets.

But that is the only way to make art" (Smithson, "Incidents").

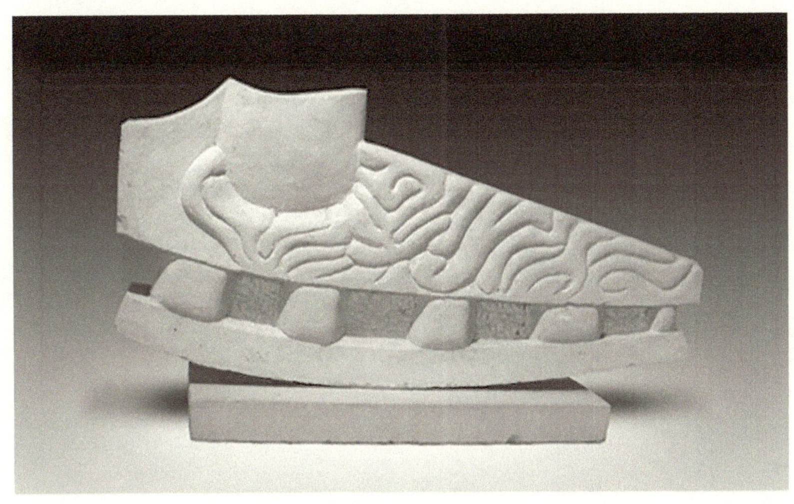

THE MOON GETS ITS ROCKS OFF ON EARTH

Aldrin: "Neal, didn't I say we might find some purple rocks?" Aldrin was now about to move the television camera. "Find the purple rocks." —Harry Holt, *For All Mankind*

The moon rocks picked up by the astronauts and brought back to earth in 1969 have shed little light on the origin of the moon. One, called the Genesis Rock, turned out to be 4.1 billion years old, roughly half a billion years older than any rock found on earth.

A result of the study of the rocks has been that scientists have gone back to an early hypothesis about the origin of the solar system, one that held that all planets were first molten bodies of rock.

Analysis of the moon rocks has shown that their chemistry is different, proving that the moon did not come from the earth. But the analysis doesn't suggest any alternatives.

And the man in the moon ain't talking!

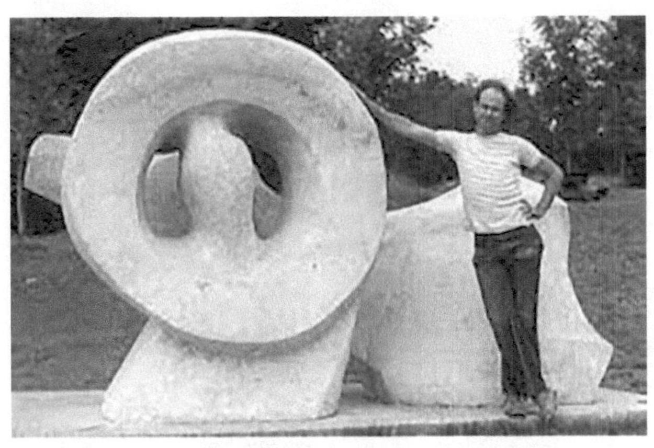

BRADFORD GRAVES was born in Wheatland, Texas, in 1939, and moved to New York City in 1958, where he studied at the School of Visual Arts, the American School of Visual Arts, and The New School, and worked as an assistant to the sculptor Alfred Van Loen, as well as for the NYC Parks Department and the Museum of Modern Art. He earned his BA and MA from Goddard College, and taught at Parsons School of Design and Fairleigh Dickinson University. Graves traveled extensively in Greece, Israel, Yugoslavia, Czechoslovakia, Spain, Iran, Afghanistan, Scotland, Senegal, Egypt, and Japan. In 1980, he was awarded an Artist's Fellowship in sculpture by the National Endowment for the Arts and created his *Crossing the Plains* sculpture for a rest area in Lincoln, Nebraska, and a Commission from the NYS Council on the Arts to create the first public sculpture on the NYS Thruway, at Schroon Lake. His work has been exhibited in both the United States and abroad. The Bradford Graves Sculpture Garden in Kerhonkson, NY, is a major repository of his work. He played saxophone in a band called Vortex, which was voted One of the Best New Bands by *CODA Magazine* in 1982, and helped launch SOUNDSCAPE with his wife, Verna Gillis, and frequently collaborated with the poets John Taggart and Michael Heller. Bradford Graves died in New York City in 1998.

http://www.bradfordgraves.com

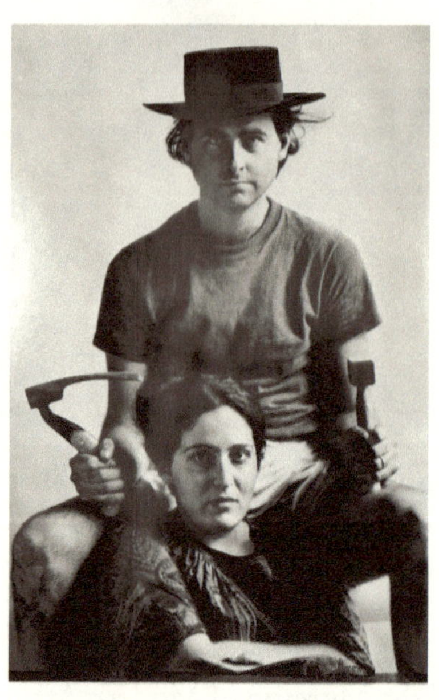

VERNA GILLIS was Brad's wife/partner for 34 years. After his death at the age of 58 she became his archivist. His work was what remained and gave her enormous solace.Together she and Brad traveled and recorded music which was released on Folkways Smithsonian Records. Verna had an active career as a music producer/manager. Since 2012 she has been writing and performing. Her one older woman's *TALES FROM GERIASSIC PARK - On the Verge of Extinction* won Best Comedic Script at the United Solo Theatre Festival in 2014. Her niche is aging. And so is she!

David Gillis, Photo, 1970.

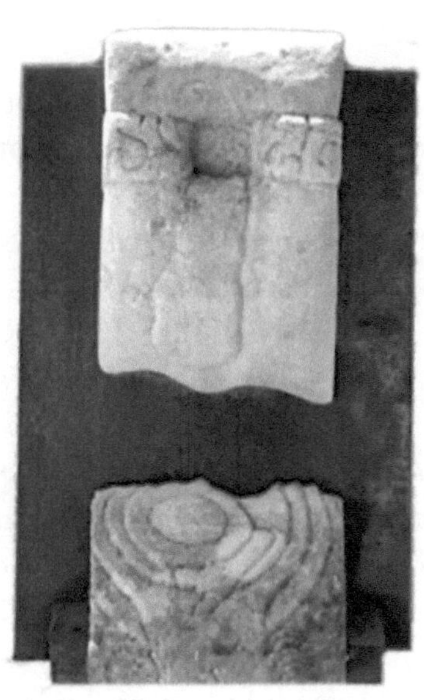

CRITICAL COMMENTARIES

The compositional schemes balance masses in a way that expresses tension between the forces of growth and gravity … I remember his past shows as being primarily of carved stone sculptures of pronounced archaic or totemic character.

EDWARD J. SOZANSKI
The Philadelphia Inquirer June 3, 2005

The limestone carvings of Bradford Graves are a celebration of profound perplexity and mystery. They explain themselves neither quickly nor easily ... Stimulating the exercise of imagination, the sculptures challenge to invent their own relevant meanings ... these silent pieces of chiseled rock plumb the sublime. In their unique way they illuminate mystical depths ... there is a growing coterie of admirers able to appreciate the majesty implicit in Graves' language of form.

BURTON WASSERMAN
ART MATTERS May, 1996

Bradford Graves is an original and ingenious form maker ... Graves' display, one of the most striking and profound sculpture solo exhibitions in Philadelphia in recent years, presents a profusion of abstract shapes that seem to well up from the artist's imagination as in natural growth.

VICTORIA DONOHOE
The Philadelphia Inquirer March 11, 1989

Bradford Graves' sculpture is complex. We see carved limestone slabs that look like the ruins of ancient walls. In front of them are horizontal pieces of limestone grooved in a geometrical pattern. One senses obscure, mystical meaning which is moving ... Graves' work is difficult to describe but very much worth seeing ... Graves is a sculptor worth following. His work is original and very interesting indeed, and the Thorpe Gallery is much to be commended for showing such radical, yet resolutely untrendy work.

JOHN CALDWELL
The New York Times March 8, 1981

Two unusually accomplished artists are now on view. Especially impressive is Bradford Graves, a sculptor who works imaginatively in limestone. Graves seems to be creating modest-sized monuments ... his work is most effective when they create the impression of almost natural elements such as one might find, perhaps, in a Surreal seaside landscape.

JAMES R. MELLOW
The New York Times May 19, 1973

Another fine display of sculpture may be seen at Georgetown University's Inter-Cultural Center and features the work of New York sculptor Bradford Graves ... More so than with the work of many modern sculptors, the viewer must rely on his intuition to interpret his pieces ... In sum, Mr. Graves' sculpture is enigmatic. It unites the twin themes of natural organic development and human-imposed structure. It succeeds. The success of this synthesis occurs on a strictly subliminal level: and it's good that it does because it keeps one thinking, questioning.

MICHAEL WEIZENBACH
The Washington Times May 1, 1986

Art galleries no longer show much carved stone sculpture which makes the show by Bradford Graves something of an anomaly. He wants it to say stone in the traditional sense, but he also tries to make it a vehicle for contemporary sculptural language. This results in work that looks a bit other worldly, as if it had dropped in from another planet ...The sculptures look archaic, like archeological artifacts. On the other hand their abstraction is organic and totally contemporary which sets up a rather vigorous clash of sensations. ... Either way, it gets your attention.

The Philadelphia Inquirer April 9, 1993

Bradford Graves sustains the greatest amount of interest through his low-keyed and highly evocative works of profound originality ... His work combines pallid, subtly textured rock with water that rests in a track-like indentation that runs down the length of limestone. The elements slowly fuse ... In other works Graves evokes his haunting rhythms, stimulating quiet contemplation of his most unusual and visionary gems of sculpture.

BARBARA CAVALIERE
arts magazine Sept., 1978

An unusually accomplished artist is now on view in the museums' galleries. Bradford Graves works imaginatively in limestone, sometimes smoothing it into seemingly weathered, slab-like shapes, sometimes breaking it up into smallish, gravel-like chunks, and sometimes even stringing it together with strands of rope. Graves' works are most effective when they create the impression of almost natural elements such as one might find, perhaps, in a Surreal seaside landscape.

ELIZABETH STEVES
The New York Times May 19, 1973

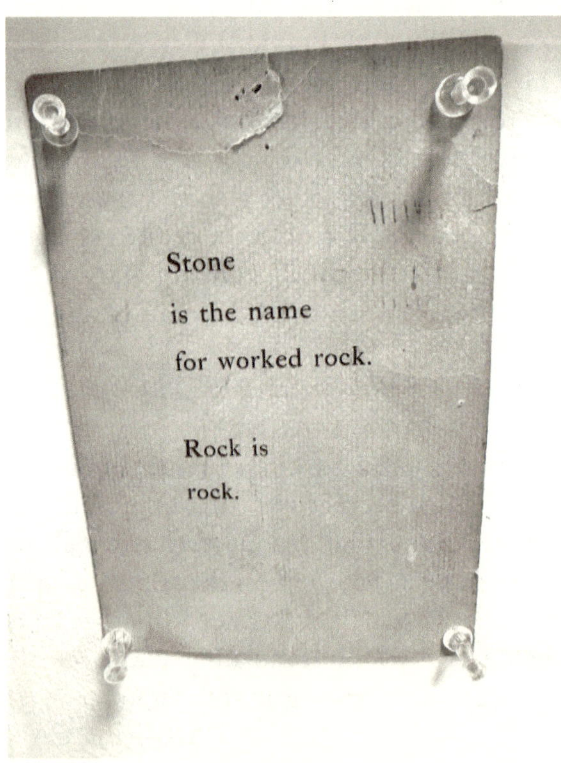

Sent from the middle of somewhere.

INDEX OF SELECTED PHOTOS/ART WORK

Blades, James. *Percussion Instruments and Their History.* Westport, CT: The Bold Strummer Ltd., 2005.

Bolton, Laura. *The Music Hunter.* New York: Doubleday, 1969.

Bord, Janet, and Colin Bord. *Mysterious Britain.* Chicago: Academy Chicago Publishing, 1974.

Bourgeois, Louise. Statement. In Dorothy Seiberling, "The Female View of Erotica," *New York Magazine,* vol. 7 (February 11, 1974).

Bronk, William. *The New World.* Rochelle, NY: Elizabeth Press, 1974.

Camus, Albert. *The Myth of Sisyphus and Other Essays.* New York: Alfred Knopf, 1983.

Freuchen, Peter. *Book of the Eskimos.* Cleveland, OH: World Publishing Company, 1961.

Geist, Sind Holt, *Brancusi: A Study of the Sculpture.* New York: Grossman, 1961.

Holt, Nancy. *Nancy Holt Interviews at Amarillo Ramp.* Holt Smithson Foundation, https://holtsmithsonfoundation.org/nancy-holt-interviews-amarillo-ramp.

Lippard, Lucy. *Six Years: The Dematerialization of the Art Object from 1966 to 1972.* Berkeley: University of California Press, 1997.

Moore, Henry. "Statement for Unit One." In *Unit One: The Modern Movement in English Architecture,* edited by Herbert Mead. London: Cassell, 1934, pp. 29–30. *Henry Moore: Sculptural Process and Public Identity,* Tate Research Publication, 2015, https://www.tate.org.uk/art/research-publications/henry-moore/henry-moore-statement-for-unit-one-r1175898.

———. *Henry Moore—Writings and Conversations.* Oakland, CA: University of California Press, 2002.

Neumann, Erich. *The Great Mother: An Analysis of the Archetype.* New York: Pantheon Books, 1963.

Partridge, Eric. *Origins: A Short Etymological Dictionary of Modern English.* New York: Routledge, 1977.

Ponge, Francis. *The Voice of Things.* New York: McGraw Hill, 1972.

Pound, Ezra. *Gaudier-Breska.* London: William Clowes and Sons, 1916.

Rank, Otto. *Art and Artist: Creative Urge and Personality.* Translated by Charles Francis Atkinson. New York: Knopf, 1932.

Roys, Ralph T. *The Book of Chilam Balam of Chumayel: Literature of the Yucatan Mayans; the Religion, Calendar and Legends of the Maya Civilization.* Great Britain, PA: Pantianos Classics, 1933.

Ryan, Peter. *Invasion of the Moon: The Story of Apollo 11.* New York: Penguin, 1969.

Sylvester, David. *Sculpture and Drawings by Henry Moore*, exhibition catalogue, Tate Gallery, London 1951.

Smithson, Robert. "Dialectic of Site and Nonsite." In *Land Art*, by Gerry Schum. Berlin, 1969.

———. "Incidents of Mirror-Travel in the Yucatan." In *Artforum* (September 1967). https://www.artforum.com/print/196907/incidents-of-mirror-travel-in-the-yucatan-36477.

———. "Towards the Development of an Air Terminal Site." 1967. https://holtsmithsonfoundation.org/towards-development-air-terminal-site.

Zim, Herbert. *Rocks and Minerals: A Guide to Familiar Minerals, Gems, Ores, and Rocks.* New York: Golden Press, 1957.

www.ingramcontent.com/pod-product-compliance
Lightning Source LLC
Chambersburg PA
CBHW022112050726
47591CB00002B/777

* 9 7 8 1 9 5 3 2 5 2 9 1 3 *